Access to Science

Other titles in the series:

Access to Citizenship

Access to History

Access to Science

Curriculum planning and practical activities
for pupils with learning difficulties

Claire Marvin and Chris Stokoe

David Fulton Publishers

London

David Fulton Publishers Ltd
The Chiswick Centre, 414 Chiswick High Road, London W4 5TF

www.fultonpublishers.co.uk

First published in Great Britain in 2003 by David Fulton Publishers. David Fulton Publishers is a division of Granada Learning Limited, part of the Granada Media group.
10 9 8 7 6 5 4 3 2 1

Note: The right of Claire Marvin and Chris Stokoe to be identified as the authors of this work has been asserted by them in accordance with the Copyright, Designs and Patents Act 1988.

British Library Cataloguing in Publication Data
A catalogue record for this book is available from the British Library.

ISBN 1–85346–917–3

Typeset by FiSH Books, London
Printed and bound in Great Britain by Ashford Colour Press, Gosport, Hants

Contents

Acknowledgements   vi

Introduction   vii

CHAPTER ONE   The importance of science for pupils with learning difficulties   1

CHAPTER TWO   Teaching approaches   17

CHAPTER THREE   The practical planning materials – how to use them   29

CHAPTER FOUR   The practical planning materials – what they are   36

CHAPTER FIVE   Practical materials – scientific enquiry   38

CHAPTER SIX   Practical materials for Key Stage 1   54

CHAPTER SEVEN   Practical materials for Key Stage 2   76

CHAPTER EIGHT   Practical materials for Key Stage 3   104

CHAPTER NINE   Practical materials for Key Stage 4   124

CHAPTER TEN   Planning for progression   138

Conclusion – meeting the challenge   143

Resources   145

References   154

Index   158

Acknowledgements

We would like to thank all those whose comments and support have encouraged us and enabled the publication of this book. For materials and photographs we thank the staff, pupils and parents of Leyland School. In particular we thank the pupils for continually challenging our thinking and providing us with the substance that nurtures our passion for and interest in inclusive education.

We would also like to thank Jude Bowen, Lesley Bush, David Hamilton, Penny Lacey and Robin Stokoe for reading and commenting on first drafts, for joining us in philosophical debate, for ICT and domestic support and for loads of inspiration, patience and understanding.

We would like to thank Widgit Software Ltd (Tel: 01223 425558) for permission to use the Rebus and PCS symbols.

Introduction

Science stimulates and excites pupils' curiosity about phenomena and events in the world around them. It also satisfies this curiosity with knowledge. Because science links direct practical experience with ideas, it can engage learners at many levels.

DfEE/QCA 1999a:15

Many adults believe that they know very little about science. This cannot be true. So much success in our daily lives depends on our use of scientific knowledge and understanding and the skills we have developed. Science is all around us and because of this, we begin to encounter and learn from scientific experiences at a very early age.

By sharing an enthusiasm for science with pupils with learning difficulties we enable them, at a simple level, to find out about what, why, when and how things happen or are likely to happen and how these events impact on their daily activities. Active approaches to learning foster exploration and investigation associated with dipping into the 'big' ideas connected with their world. This can all take place with a sense of fun in a stimulating yet familiar environment. Children learn best when they are enjoying themselves and teaching too becomes so much more pleasurable!

About this book

The following statements underpin our practice and define the priorities for this book. In addition they introduce the reader to our enthusiasm for, and commitment to, science-focused teaching and learning that is fundamental to the text. Based on our experience of teaching pupils of all ages and abilities in mainstream and specialist settings we believe that science, for pupils with learning difficulties:

- provides an accessible and stimulating context and content for the planning of challenging learning opportunities
- can be accessed through a variety of teaching approaches including play
- offers opportunities for first-hand investigative learning with all pupils having equality of access to a wide range of experiences and activities.

Written to motivate and support colleagues who work with pupils with learning difficulties this book is about improving access to science. Its content is intended to help teachers accept responsibility for the individual learning of all pupils in their school by preparing them to teach those pupils confidently in an exciting, imaginative and playful context. It is concerned with promoting positive participation for all, within learning experiences and environments which reflect the interests and achievements of every learner. To this end the book complements and reinforces the key principles for developing a more inclusive curriculum – setting suitable learning challenges, responding to pupils' diverse learning needs and overcoming potential barriers to learning – set out in the National Curriculum handbook (DfEE/QCA 1999b: 30).

Supported throughout by examples based on the authors' experiences of teaching pupils with learning difficulties *Access to Science* is a practical guide to teaching science as part of the whole school curriculum. Its main aim is to support staff who work with pupils with learning difficulties to:

- set developmentally appropriate and challenging learning targets for individual pupils within the context of science
- plan for and implement imaginative, science-focused activities based on the four areas of science that constitute the programmes of study set out in the National Curriculum
- define assessment and recording opportunities and methods.

Four chapters precede the practical materials. Chapter 1 describes the issues surrounding the inclusion of science in the early editions of the National Curriculum and its development through subsequent revisions of content. Consideration of the importance of teaching science to pupils with learning difficulties follows. In Chapter 2 a range of relevant teaching methods are described, and how they help to create opportunities for accessible and effective learning and teaching. A detailed description of the practical materials, that make up the core of the book, is presented in Chapter 3 and Chapter 4 carries a brief introduction to them.

Chapter 5 precedes the key stage-specific practical section. It presents an overview of the skills and procedures that underpin scientific investigation and provides examples of how these skills are taught through contexts taken from the content dimension of science. Chapters 6 to 9 contain the practical materials – one chapter for each key stage. Each one begins with a description of appropriate learning for pupils in a specific key stage based on the QCA/DfEE (2001a) guidelines booklet *Planning, Teaching and Assessing the Curriculum for Pupils with Learning Difficulties – Science*, which includes the latest performance descriptions (P levels). This is followed by examples of medium-term plans for science-focused units of work covered over a term or half a term, a planning sheet for a series of weekly lessons devised from a selected unit of work and a short-term plan that exemplifies a single session from within the series. Comprehensive and accessible suggestions for resources specific to units of work support this planning advice.

Chapter 10 describes and exemplifies the complex process of planning for progression of curriculum content and experiences. General resources, including blank planning sheet formats, are listed at the end of the book.

We appreciate that not all readers will wish to or have time to read the whole book. We have therefore designed it for selective reading with most chapters and sections of chapters self-contained but usefully cross-referenced. In order to bring meaning and relevance to the practical materials however it is hoped that readers will familiarise themselves with the explanations and suggestions in Chapter 3.

Terminology

Throughout the text an emphasis has been placed on providing access to science for the widest audience in terms of both readers of this book and pupils with learning difficulties. To this end the use of appropriate vocabulary has been carefully considered since some terminology may introduce inappropriate messages or simply put readers off! In order to meet these concerns the description 'learning difficulties' has been used to describe the full range of moderate, severe and profound and multiple learning difficulties which may relate to pupils aged from two to post-16.

The term 'pupil' has been used throughout to indicate our concern that access to scientific activities should not be tied to any one age group. In addition the terms 'practitioner' and 'teacher' are used interchangeably and taken to imply anyone with a teaching role in a range of provision which includes early years, mainstream and specialist settings in the maintained and independent sectors.

The book is practical in nature – its core (Chapters 5–9) providing guidance and ideas for the planning and implementation of science-focused units of work. Where this core section is referred to in the text the term 'practical materials' is used throughout.

Health and safety

Most pupils display a natural curiosity and desire to explore their environment. In school this should be encouraged but, at the same time, pupils must not be placed in dangerous or harmful situations. To ensure pupil safety practitioners have a responsibility to familiarise themselves with and implement health and safety guidelines. This involves the undertaking of regular risk assessment within and outside the classroom. Local authority and school-based health and safety officers have a responsibility to monitor and review procedures from time to time. In addition to their support practitioners may obtain advice from national organisations and their regular journals and newsletters (see Resources).

Pupils should be made aware of the risks associated with science-focused activities and supported in carrying them out as safely as possible. A general statement on those aspects of health and safety to be taught to pupils is included in the National Curriculum booklet for science (DfEE/QCA 1999a). While parts of the content may be too demanding for some pupils with learning difficulties, they learn by observing and imitating the actions of peers and adults, therefore members of the staff team should always model good practice and maintain rigorous safety routines.

CHAPTER ONE

The importance of science for pupils with learning difficulties

'We're trying to make them shoot. Press that button over there. It went whoosh, it went pop!'

Playing with syringes and investigating changes in pressure. Daniel, Year 6

This chapter brings the reader up-to-date with the issues surrounding the inclusion of science in the National Curriculum. This is followed by a justification for teaching science to pupils with learning difficulties and a brief description of the content of the science programmes of study together with a consideration of their relevance for pupils with learning difficulties.

Science in the National Curriculum

Before the introduction of the National Curriculum in 1989 (DES 1988) science was regarded as an optional extra in many primary and special schools despite government intentions to introduce 'science for all' in an earlier policy document (DES 1985). So, in 1989, it came as a surprise to most teachers when the subject was elevated to the status of 'core subject' alongside English and mathematics – an added importance greeted by many with apprehension and restraint (Ritchie 2001). Further difficulties arose as a result of Her Majesty's Inspectorate reporting inadequate provision for teaching science in special schools (HMI 1986, 1990). Practitioners felt that attempting to teach scientific concepts to pupils with learning difficulties would be an irrelevant addition to the school day, fuelled in part by lack of resources and by their own feelings of inadequacy for the accompanying subject knowledge and understanding. As Coltman (1996: 243) suggested:

> a common response when matters of science are raised during adult conversation is a total shut down. Many of us have an antipathy to the subject founded on hours spent in school laboratories which smelled of coal gas ... and a teacher who presented incomprehensible hypotheses attributed to a cavalcade of assorted historical personae.

Many years on from the introduction of the National Curriculum, and despite a continuing lack of confidence in how best to teach scientific knowledge and understanding (Bell 1998), few practitioners appear to question the validity of science for pupils with learning difficulties. The publication and subsequent revisions of the materials have had a major impact on curriculum development in schools. The entitlement of all pupils to a balanced and broadly-based curriculum is now fully accepted. In addition much work has been done in individual settings to build on the principles of inclusion (DfEE/QCA 1999b) that replace and extend the statements on access in earlier editions (DfE 1995). Schools have been encouraged to develop their own inclusive school curriculum in ways that match their aims, meet the varied needs of their pupils and fulfil statutory requirements. In the same way this has included careful consideration of the relevance of individual subjects of the National Curriculum.

In order to give all pupils appropriately challenging experiences and learning opportunities associated with individual or linked subjects, processes for modifying the programmes of study were described in several early documents (NCC 1992a, SCAA 1996). More recently they are considered and exemplified in the QCA/DfEE guidelines *Planning, Teaching and Assessing the Curriculum for Pupils with Learning Difficulties* (2001a, b, c). Written collaboratively by practitioners and experts in the field these materials draw on effective practice across a range of schools and offer long awaited yet comprehensive support to the range of services that support pupils with learning difficulties. For these reasons the guidelines are frequently referred to in this book.

It is our belief that science is now one of the success stories of the National Curriculum, a view supported by findings from reports of inspections in mainstream and specialist settings (Ofsted 2001). The teaching of science, it is noted, has improved significantly in over 40 per cent of schools, and in the majority of special schools pupils 'make satisfactory or better progress'. Despite these encouraging results however, the same document states that many special schools are struggling to achieve a satisfactory balance between subjects and an insufficient amount of teaching time is allocated to science. Government initiatives, for example the literacy, numeracy and Key Stage 3 curriculum strategies, added to lack of guidance on balancing different curriculum components, contribute to these tensions.

Encouragingly the QCA/DfEE (2001b) *General guidelines* have been designed to provide support for curriculum organisation. Taking account of several factors, for example, their own school aims, the needs of the pupils attending the school and the requirements to provide a broad and balanced curriculum (which includes the subjects of the National Curriculum and RE) the guidelines state that it is for individual schools to determine and justify the amount of time allocated to different parts of the curriculum. Decisions about balance and time, as well as breadth, will need to be continually reviewed and revised in light of pupils' changing individual needs. In support of this guidance, Lawson *et al.* (2001) suggest that schools may now feel more confident in allocating time to curriculum components. Future inspection reports will, no doubt, record the progress in this direction.

Thinking and learning – the relationship to science

Learning and development in humans is so complex that no single theory can adequately account for all the interrelated processes involved. While detailed explanations can be found elsewhere (for example Donaldson 1978, Fontana 1995, Wood 1998), put simply there are several accepted principles fundamental to learning which relate to all children. Learning is usually an active and, initially, sensory process that often takes place in a social context. By acting on the world, sometimes alongside a more experienced other, the child develops anticipation and understanding of actions and events that represent the beginning of taking control of their environment. For example, if a baby notices that a mobile placed over his cot moves when he happens to strike the cot side he will, after a period of time, *intend* to produce this *anticipated* result through his own actions.

Meaningful contexts help children to make sense of new experiences and learning opportunities by relating them to what they already know. They hypothesise, experiment, test the theory, discard it or accept it and thus go on to develop further personal theories. Most children are enthusiastically curious by nature and like to be challenged and excited by an environment that encourages exploration and discovery, whether with assistance or independently.

Ryan

Ryan is in the playground on a windy day in autumn. He runs around kicking the leaves and trying to catch them. He pauses every now and then to pick some up and he puts them in his pocket. After a while he stops running and goes over to one of the trees that are shedding their leaves, and reaches up to the branches, looking carefully. He can't reach so he gets one of his collected leaves out of his pocket and begins a game of throwing it in the air and trying to catch it again. He watches the wind whip the leaf away and chases it laughing.

Ryan already knows that leaves come from trees when he sees them attached to the branches. Now he is beginning to make the connection that the leaves on the ground have come from the trees by being blown off in the wind. He then imitates the wind by throwing them up in the air.

As stated in the introduction, we believe that first-hand, concrete, science-focused experiences provide an exceptional opportunity for learning. To justify this statement we have first examined the ways in which children learn. A consideration of the relevance of these principles to the content of the science programmes of study and to pupils with learning difficulties follows next.

Requirements of the science curriculum

The statutory content of the curriculum – pupils' entitlement to science – is outlined in the programmes of study for the National Curriculum (DfEE/QCA 1999a), and, for pre-Key Stage 1 pupils, the early learning goals, although not statutory, set out what might reasonably be expected of pupils in the foundation stage (QCA/DfEE 1999, 2000). Long-term planning for units of work may involve reference to both documents in addition to accredited schemes, and to local and national initiatives (see Chapter 3).

The programmes of study state that there are two main aspects of a balanced science curriculum:

- enquiring scientifically (the process dimension) and
- knowledge and understanding (the content dimension).

The following section describes their key elements and their relevance for pupils with learning difficulties.

Scientific enquiry

Scientific enquiry (Sc1) permeates all aspects of the programmes of study. It is not an activity in itself but rather a way of approaching all activities. Described in the previous paragraph on how children learn, it is to observe, explore, discover, investigate and problem solve, to predict, revise and finally to obtain and consider evidence. It is a *process* which includes the skills, strategies and attitudes for learning, the skills that underpin all scientific experiences and most learning opportunities. More importantly these skills can be transferred across subject boundaries, across the curriculum and to

Using scientific enquiry skills to investigate materials

Week by week, during a series of lessons on freezing and melting (Figure 1.1), a group of Key Stage 1 pupils with a range of learning difficulties pour coloured water into some cut-down plastic bottles (Figure 1.1a). They help carry them to the freezer where they are stored. Each week using their available senses, the pupils touch, observe, comment on and compare the results of their previous activity (Figure 1.1b) until, finally, the bottles are full of coloured layers of ice. The teacher, Mrs Alfa, wants the pupils to explore the properties of the ice and to compare it with water so she asks a series of questions to encourage the pupils to think about how to release the ice from the containers, for example: 'I want to feel the ice, can we get it out of the bottle?' 'Will the ice turn to water?' (Figure 1.1c).

1.1a Pouring the next layer of coloured water into the bottles

1.1b Exploring and commenting on the contents

1.1c Discussing the results – the pupils sign 'cold'

1.1d Trying out ways to melt the ice

Figure 1.1 Scientific enquiry at Key Stage 1

Supported by a variety of resources to prompt discussion the pupils suggest strategies to get the ice out of the bottles and to melt it, for example, hair dryer, hammer, warm water, put the bottles outside, electric fan. Within reason the pupils are encouraged to try these out, record the method, predict and comment on the effect (Figure 1.1d). Subsequently Mrs Alfa helps the pupils interpret the results and draw conclusions from their evidence. As a group they decide that the most controlled methods of melting the ice are certainly the safest but definitely not the most exciting!

life outside and beyond school. Encouragingly the QCA/DfEE (2001a: 4) guidelines for science demonstrate the significance of the development and practice of these skills and procedures by stating that, in particular, science offers the pupils opportunities to:

- develop an awareness of, and interest in, themselves and their immediate surroundings and environment
- join in practical activities that link to ideas, *for example doing and thinking*
- use their senses to explore and investigate
- develop an understanding of cause and effect.

Within a government climate of enthusiasm for testing and target setting it is easy to lose sight of the importance of process in favour of product. Pressures to collect evidence of pupil progress, to relate this to targets and to the school improvement cycle (QCA/DfEE 2001d) are a reality. Yet for all pupils the ability to develop, utilise and refine thinking processes which lead to understanding remains essential. It is vitally important that the skills and strategies associated with scientific enquiry, for example, observation, questioning and problem solving, retain their prominence and underpin all activities (NCC 1992a, DfEE/QCA 1999a). The aim of this approach, Collis and Lacey (1996) suggest, is to develop understanding through effective interaction with the materials, natural phenomena and the social environment.

Knowledge and understanding of science

Science provides a means of gaining knowledge and understanding about the world through the process of scientific enquiry. The three remaining sections of the programmes of study set out the existing knowledge and understanding that pupils should be taught at each key stage. Under the headings of:

- *Life processes and living things* (Sc2) (see Figure 1.2)
- *Materials and their properties* (Sc3) (see Figure 1.3)
- *Physical processes* (Sc4) (see Figure 1.4)

 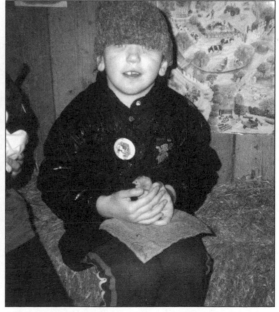

1.2a Animals need food and water and   **1.2b** to be treated with care and sensitivity

Figure 1.2 Learning about life processes and living things

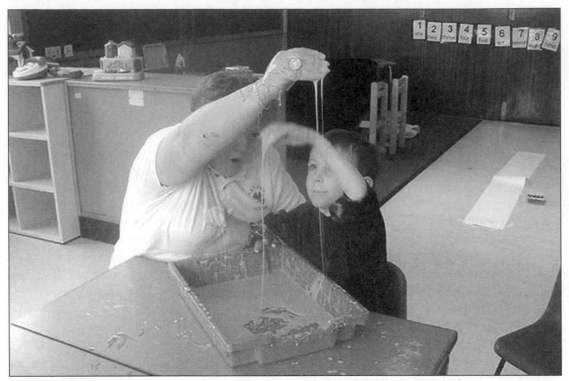

Figure 1.3 Learning about materials and their properties – exploring a change of state

Figure 1.4 Learning about physical processes – push or pull?

these sections identify the areas of science which provide the *content* dimension – the common framework around which individual schools can develop units of work.

Further description related to how the content of these areas represents appropriate learning for pupils with diverse needs at each key stage and practical ideas for teaching that include the development of skills and attitudes associated with *Scientific enquiry* (Sc1), can be found in the practical materials (see Chapters 5–9).

The importance of subject knowledge

Conclusions from research in mainstream settings (Alexander *et al.* 1992, Bennett and Carré 1993, Russell *et al.* 1994) and the views of experts (Jones and Skelton 1993, Marshall and Palacio 1997) suggest that teachers' knowledge and understanding of the scientific ideas set out in the content dimension of the programmes of study is of key importance to effective teaching and learning. While science may pose particular problems in this area we believe that these findings contribute to a much broader debate about the role of subject knowledge in education (Hollins and Whitby 2001).

Traditionally, possessing subject expertise has been characteristic of secondary school teachers, while in primary education inspectors' reports allude to its absence (Ofsted 1998). For those teachers trained in primary school practice a requirement to understand the knowledge, skills and processes which characterise each and every National Curriculum subject is a tall order, but not a reason to despair. A common entitlement to high quality learning opportunities derived from core and foundation subjects has undoubtedly brought advantages for pupils with learning difficulties. The subjects promote balance and breadth of study and provide interesting contexts of experience for learning, therefore they should be planned with rigour. Teachers cannot expect to be a leading authority on every subject in a school curriculum but they can make sure they have a basic grasp of the key principles within the topics they set out to teach. We believe that most practitioners, with the support of a school's science leader, can achieve this and, in turn, provide pupils with effective opportunities for learning throughout their school career.

What is most important is to match the content of science, with care, to the needs, interests and past experiences of the pupils. The task of the practitioner is to respond to pupil diversity while bearing in mind their entitlement to a range of curriculum opportunities. Pupils with learning difficulties learn at a slower rate and planning for content will need to be more selective. The majority are unlikely to make measurable progress towards the abstract and the scientific and some aspects of the programmes of study at Key Stage 1 will remain relevant into adult life (NCC 1992a, Jones and Skelton 1993, Lawson *et al.* 2001). Perhaps most appropriate to the pupils in question is the study of everyday aspects of science and their application to independent living, while access to the rich and varied content of the later key stages creates breadth and depth of experience and maintains interest and motivation.

While the possession of *basic* subject knowledge is important for teachers of pupils with learning difficulties, the *context* of science as well as the *content* offers essential opportunities for relevant and meaningful learning. Within a scientific framework, the skills and concepts associated with learning how to learn, for example, using the senses, questioning, the ability to problem solve, can be practised and consolidated as can the key skills and other priority areas of learning embedded in pupils' individual education plans (IEPs) (see section on key skills later in this chapter). Addressing these essential aspects of learning at the same time as scientific content may prove to be, as Byers (1999) suggests, the most productive and valuable way forward for curriculum development. This approach recognises the possibility of pupils gaining science-specific knowledge and understanding and should not be overlooked. After all if pupils are learning to use key cross-curricular skills to enable effective thinking it is equally important that they have something to think about!

Similarities and differences

A group of Year 5 pupils with a range of learning difficulties are working together. They explore a range of interesting objects pulled from a feely-bag, for example, a wooden carving, perfumed candle, plastic toy, glass ornament and cooking utensils. Using science as a context and according to their individual needs they also learn to sit with the group, take turns, listen respectfully to others' comments and share the resources with their peers.

After a while each pupil chooses a favourite object. With these out of sight their attention is drawn to the properties of two unusual items placed on the table in front of them. Kieran, for example, notices that one is made of wood and 'it's hard'. Then, with appropriate support, the pupils match their own objects to those on the table. Two distinct groups emerge – articles made of wood and those made of metal. Now it's Fatima's turn. She picks up her object – a salad server with a metal bowl and a wooden handle – and comments 'cold', 'shiny', 'it's metal', while placing it in the 'metal' group. The teaching assistant encourages her to 'look again, look carefully'. With surprise Fatima notices 'it's wood as well'. She continues 'put it in the middle' – and so a subset is formed.

Within this activity Fatima is developing and consolidating science-specific knowledge and understanding in addition to key cross-curricular skills that provide priority areas for her learning. She learns to wait for her turn, to pay attention and to share, while at the same time demonstrating that she can group the salad server according to its origins, name the materials from which it is made and describe some simple properties.

The role of the subject leader

Teachers of pupils with learning difficulties, as suggested above, are expected to make judgements with regard to the fine balance between a focus upon subject content and individual needs. In addition they must confirm their knowledge of the principles and justifications underlying the activities introduced, however simple. Research has shown that subject leaders can be an effective support in resolving these complex issues (Kelly 1997), more especially to colleagues whose experience or confidence in delivering a subject is limited. In a fully developed curriculum model most pupils will be working simultaneously towards a range of outcomes, both cross-curricular and subject-focused, and the subject leader can add informed support to the inevitable balancing act taking place.

Developed in consultation with a broad range of professionals concerned with education, the *National Standards for Subject Leaders* published by the Teacher Training Agency (1998), define the expertise demanded of this role. Over and above that of class teacher, they state that subject leaders should be able to:

- offer advice and encouragement to colleagues
- inform, monitor and evaluate teaching and learning
- review and update the science scheme of work and teaching resources
- liaise with other subject leaders and the senior leadership team.

With heavy demands on their time, therefore, teachers in this role are seeking effective methods of disseminating expertise and supporting colleagues. One indirect but efficient way of doing so is through the school's scheme of work for science. Often developed and reviewed by the science leader, individual units of work may contain a 'points to note'. This short section explains possible conceptual difficulties that pupils and teachers may have and sets out other specific points to remember when teaching the unit, for example, in relation to health and safety. Of particular use to those teachers with limited experience, this method represents one way of providing guidance and support, while at the same time ensuring that practices improve the quality of education provided and meet the individual needs of pupils.

Cross-curricular links

The essentially practical way that most of science should be taught demonstrates a unique opportunity to link the environment and our surroundings to every part of the curriculum, thus sharing common content, consolidating skills and stimulating new learning. Since there is no requirement to teach the subjects of the National Curriculum separately and considerable demands are made on teaching time in schools, selected subjects can be accessed by linking units of work. There is considerable help available to achieve this task in the National Curriculum documents and schemes of work (DfEE/QCA 1998, 1999a, 2000), the QCA/DfEE (2001a) science booklet and the practical materials in this book. Examples of the many links that science-focused experiences and activities can make with other subjects are presented in Table 1.1.

Cross-curricular links

A mixed-ability class of Key Stage 3 and 4 pupils with severe and profound and multiple learning difficulties are carrying out an investigation into light sources. They are studying the 1940s in history and therefore historical forms of light are included, for example, an oil lamp and a candle. In turn they shine light sources on to an adult face and make group decisions as to their effectiveness. Results are recorded on a prepared worksheet.

Midway through the lesson, in semi-darkness and without the knowledge of the pupils, the teaching assistant turns on a recording of an air raid warning siren. Some pupils respond immediately – they get under the tables and check the window blinds – others require help to recall what is expected of them. During the 'air raid' the group decide that a tea light would be appropriate illumination. Before the teaching assistant sneaks out again to sound the 'all clear' they recall the story they are reading in English about a boy who is evacuated in the Blitz (*Goodnight Mr Tom* by Michelle Magorian) and discuss what it must have felt like to have been a child in those times.

Having considered its effectiveness the pupils decide to put on the electric light for the plenary. Together they talk about the evidence they have collected. With skilful support and questioning they make simple comparisons between historical light sources and modern equivalents.

Establishing effective cross-curricular links demands careful planning and skilful teaching that, in turn, contributes to effective strategies for managing time and the different components in the curriculum at each key stage (Ofsted 2002). While learning

Table 1.1 Examples of cross-curricular links

Subject	Examples of links
English speaking and listening	• body movements, gestures, vocalisation and speech promoted by exciting activities or interesting sensory objects • group discussion related to prediction, investigation, reporting results
reading	• reading 'lists' of required resources – may be objects, pictures, symbols or written words accessed visually, orally or through touch • matching pictures, symbols and words to materials, objects and living things during sorting and grouping activities
writing	• predicting outcomes using a preferred method of recording • participating in investigations, for example, finding photographs of themselves to record their participation • presenting evidence
Mathematics number	• using developing awareness to predict change • counting linked to scientific enquiry and comparison of quantity, for example, *more* pupils liked the vanilla ice cream during a unit of work on freezing and melting, estimating the number of items and using counting to confirm • making sets, for example, according to common properties of materials
shape, space and measure	• making direct comparisons using non-standard or standard measures, for example, the height of beans, the distance travelled when cars are pushed down a ramp, the weight of natural materials • understanding measures, for example, filling containers to make different sounds, scooping up pebbles/feathers and comparing materials
handling data	• using numerical information to solve scientific problems • using a list, sorting circles or a block graph to represent the results of an investigation
ICT	• using switches to control objects and events, for example, a tape recorder to identify their own voices and familiar sounds • accessing computer programs, for example, to classify objects, to stimulate interest and excitement such as viewing a moving skeleton or the rotation of the Earth • symbolically recording results of investigations • using communication aids to make predictions, choices
Art and design	• exploring, investigating, combining and changing materials, for example, choosing and grouping shiny and dull materials before making a collage, using available senses to explore and then manipulate materials such as dough and clay, observing materials change (such as plaster of Paris) • painting and printing with body parts and having opportunities to identify and name them • contrasting light and dark • recording observations of the world around them, for example, *looking* closely at a flower and sketching it

Table 1.1 continued

Subject	Examples of links
PSHE and citizenship	• taking control by planning, organising and carrying out own investigations • caring for living things • preparing for and coping with change, for example, sequencing photographs of the life cycle of pets, puberty • developing a healthy lifestyle • identifying and respecting similarities and differences between people

Geography	• using enquiry skills, for example:
	  – exploring and observing the immediate or wider surroundings using available senses
	  – collecting and sorting natural objects in the local environment
	  – comparing local environments, for example, town and country parks
	  – exploring, observing and investigating the elements, for example, water, wind
	  – observing and comparing the differences in the physical features of humans

History	• experiencing and commenting on the passage of time, for example, how they have changed, the human life cycle and their immediate families
Music	• creating sounds spontaneously, for example, vocal, body percussion or use of home made 'instruments' • identifying and naming parts of the body through songs • exploring and classifying instruments according to materials, for example, wooden, metallic • listening to mammal noises, bird song • using sounds descriptively to describe scientific experiences, activities and investigations

Design and technology	• designing and making resources, for example, noise makers, waterproof hats
	• acquiring the knowledge, skills and understanding associated with the above, for example:
	  – joining and fastening plastic cups and string to make a telephone
	  – making simple circuits for meaningful use
	  – comparing the insulating properties of materials
	• exploring and investigating familiar products using available senses, for example:
	  – comparing the changes in fruit over time
	  – comparing uncooked ingredients and baked cake
	  – winding mechanisms that include pulleys and gears
	  – making drinks and simple meals by dissolving, melting, heating and cooling (changes of state) of materials

Physical education	• experiencing and showing awareness of the range and quality of whole-body movements, for example, balancing, travelling, rolling, jumping • gaining experience and knowledge of health-related fitness, for example, awareness of changes to the body when active, knowing about different types of exercise • experiencing forces and motion through swimming, gymnastics, games and dance

opportunities become seamless, holistic, coherent experiences for pupils, teachers need to ensure that they maintain a clear view of the knowledge, skills and understanding related to specific subjects and how it links together. If science is deemed the 'host' subject, the essence of science must be maintained throughout, by reinforcement of scientific concepts and planning for subject-specific assessment opportunities. Incidental learning however should not be ignored. The most significant outcomes in classrooms, both positive and negative, are often unplanned (Collis and Lacey 1996). Figure 1.5 shows Key Stage 4 pupils practising and extending key skills while investigating the transmission of sound during a science-focused unit of work linked to design and technology and mathematics.

Figure 1.5 Investigating the transmission of sound

Developing key skills and other transferable skills

Described and exemplified in the National Curriculum (DfEE/QCA 1999b) and further elaborated in the *Developing skills* booklet (QCA/DfEE 2001c) the key skill areas, thinking skills and additional skills, which may form priority areas for learning, can often be best addressed in the context of subject-focused group activities. This approach enables specific experiences to be designed in response to each pupil's individual needs and increases the level of relevance in the curriculum experience (Carpenter and Ashdown 2001).

As previously stated, science should not be seen as a subject in isolation but one which interrelates with many more subjects and other aspects of the whole curriculum. It is our belief that the practical, investigative and playful nature of science makes it an ideal platform for developing, practising, refining, generalising and combining these skills. Although not an exhaustive list, Table 1.2 provides examples of key skills in the context of science. Tables 1.3 and 1.4 set out the thinking skills and additional skills, respectively, that may also form priority areas of learning. Figure 1.6 shows Key Stage 2 pupils using science as a context for the development of key skills and thinking skills such as sensory awareness, communication, problem solving, working with others and prediction.

Table 1.2 Key skills for learning in the context of science

Skill area	Science contexts in which pupils can develop, maintain, refine, consolidate and generalise key skills
Communication	may include: • responding to and interacting with others using a preferred method of communication, for example, facial expression and gesture, through the use of photographs, pictures, symbols and signing or the spoken word • communicating effectively and appropriately in changing contexts • emerging literacy skills, for example, making a class book about flowers or a journey into space using a preferred method of recording
Application of number	may include: • exploring and manipulating objects – to encourage understanding of object permanence • matching, sorting, grouping, comparing and classifying objects and materials • recognising, interpreting, predicting and estimating through practical activities involving enquiry • collecting and presenting data, for example, household appliances that provide heat or those that keep items cold • looking for patterns
Information technology	may include: • using ICT to engage with the environment and to promote independence, for example, using a switch to operate an ice-making machine, communicating with adults and peers • using software packages to obtain information and to handle data recorded during investigations
Working with others	may include: • tolerating others within their personal space, turn-taking, sharing, negotiating and supporting • recognising a common purpose by working collaboratively to obtain a result, for example, planning, setting up and carrying out an investigation with another pupil or group of pupils
Improving own learning and performance	may include: • realising and indicating needs, wants, preferences • recognising why a task is carried out and what it involves, for example, making jellies in order to observe changes in state by carrying out a fair test • recognising the completion of a task • evaluating the results of an activity
Problem solving	may include: • exploring and manipulating objects – to encourage understanding of cause and effect • planning, carrying out and reviewing investigations by using appropriate strategies, for example, a symbolic or written plan • recognising – with support – when strategies need changing

Table 1.3 Thinking skills

Effective thinking is made up of a complex web of related skills and structures. An impairment in any one area may hinder the process as a whole. Alongside the key skills described and exemplified in Table 1.2, those skills which contribute to successful thinking may form priority areas of learning for pupils with learning difficulties and can be addressed in scientific contexts. Examples are included below but a more detailed explanation of early developmental skills can be found in Wood (1998), Fisher (1995) and Ashman and Conway (1989).

Thinking skills	include: • sensory awareness and perception • anticipating and predicting outcomes • remembering • understanding cause and effect • linking objects, events and experiences • creative and imaginative thinking, for example, suggesting and looking for alternative outcomes • reasoning, for example, giving reasons for actions • enquiry skills, for example, asking questions, investigating • evaluation skills

Table 1.4 Additional priority areas for learning

Science-focused activities provide appropriate experiences and learning contexts in which to develop, practise, extend and generalise those additional skills which may also form priority areas of learning. Examples are included below.

Physical orientation and mobility skills	include: • fine motor skills • positioning skills
Organisation and study skills	include: • directing and focusing attention • sustaining interest and motivation
Personal and social skills	include: • managing their own behaviour • managing their own emotions
Daily living skills	include: • domestic skills, for example, using electrical appliances safely
Leisure and recreation skills	include: • choosing between familiar activities in school, for example, science resources – magnets, magnifying glasses – and favourite books • using community facilities to promote healthy living

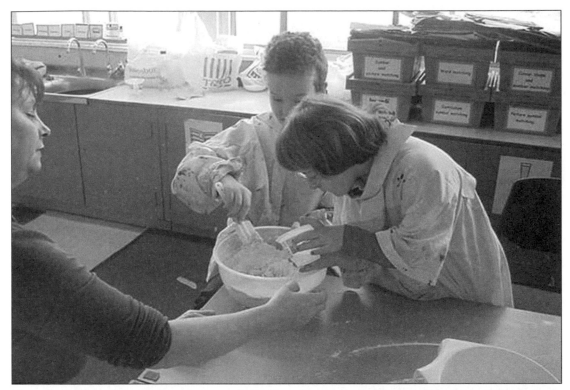

Figure 1.6 Using science as a context Key Stage 2 pupils develop key skills and thinking skills

The sensory circus

Following a whole-class introduction, that includes recall of past experiences and investigations, some Key Stage 2 pupils with learning difficulties take part in a science circus – the penultimate lesson from a unit of work on *Our senses*. They visit five prepared areas, each one containing exciting resources to encourage problem solving and the use of a particular sense. There are several tasks to complete. Working in groups and supported by an adult, most pupils respond to and explore the materials. Together they discuss the sense best represented in that area and select an appropriate symbol for display. Before moving on, each pupil selects a favourite activity, locates a corresponding picture-symbol and matches and sticks it to a relevant column on a bar chart. The group look at the data, discuss the emerging trends, then suggest the next area. A few pupils carry a prompt sheet to enable them to work independently. Using this as a guide they recognise what is involved, complete appropriate tasks and progress without support.

At the end of the lesson the class come together again. To aid recall pupils point to and/or name the home-made sensory 'models' on display in the classroom. The bar charts are evaluated and simple conclusions drawn.

Within the science-focused sensory circus pupils have been encouraged to develop and extend the following key skills and thinking skills:

* *communication*, for example, interacting and communicating with others, the application of emerging literacy skills

- *application of number*, for example, interpreting and presenting data

- *information technology*, for example, using switches to access resources

- *working with others*, for example, turn-taking and sharing

- *improving own learning performance*, for example, following a prompt sheet and recognising when to move on

- *problem solving*, for example, deciding which sensory area to visit next

- *thinking skills*, for example, deciding the sense best represented in each area.

Summary

Learning is complex and can be particularly challenging for pupils with learning difficulties yet science is now accepted as an exciting practical-based subject, which can provide access to all or some of the following:

- experiences and opportunities for learning knowledge, skills and understanding critical to the subject of science
- key skills, thinking skills and additional priority areas of learning
- other subjects or curriculum areas.

Supported by science leaders successful learning is in the hands of skilful practitioners – practitioners who can demonstrate the ability to plan in such a way that individual pupil targets are addressed in the context of science-focused experiences and activities that link rigorously to other subjects. Progress for individual pupils may take place in many areas and teachers should remain open to and aware of them all.

CHAPTER TWO

Teaching approaches

'Paper cup might work; you make hole; yes, I'll put string in; do you want long or short?'

Making a telephone exchange. Tina, Year 11

When planning the delivery of science-focused experiences and activities practitioners differentiate their teaching approaches to meet the needs of particular pupil groups and the particular needs, abilities and preferences of individual pupils. The QCA/DfEE guidelines (2001b: 20) suggest that teachers will draw on a range of teaching approaches including:

- broad perspectives, *for example, behavioural or interactive*
- particular techniques, *for example, prompting, shaping or questioning*
- specific ways of working in the classroom, *for example, investigation, exploration, working together as a group or role play.*

This chapter begins with an overall consideration of teaching approaches relevant to science and subsequently examines two in greater detail.

It is our experience that most methods described in the guidelines (QCA/DfEE 2001b) can be used effectively to provide learning opportunities in science-focused activities. For most pupils with learning difficulties these approaches will involve a significant and ongoing sensory dimension across the key stages (Marvin 1998, QCA/DfEE 2001b, Dorchester Curriculum Group 2002). For example, the ability to observe is not only important for the development of early learning skills but also for scientific enquiry. The term 'observation' is intended here not to mean exclusively using the sense of sight. Where possible all available senses should be involved so that pupils with learning difficulties gain greater familiarity with and understanding of their surroundings. For some pupils it will mean their immediate surroundings and only a manageable amount of sensory input presented at any one time, for others a wider environment where careful observations and measurements are made, for example of plant growth or lengths of shadows at certain times in the day.

In order to offer pupils a well-balanced and varied range of experiences and learning opportunities it is important to use a selection of teaching approaches according to how best they learn. Active learning and investigation are core elements of scientific enquiry but for pupils with learning difficulties many of the processes and skills involved, for example, planning, predicting, drawing conclusions, will prove difficult to master and present enormous barriers to learning (Tilstone *et al.* 2000). There is much that practitioners can do however to encourage and support their learning. Two approaches that we believe are both essential and successful are described in greater detail below – questioning and play.

Questioning

Teaching pupils with learning difficulties to use questioning as a learning strategy is complex but important, and essential to the process of scientific enquiry. Both (1997) reminds his readers that the interaction of children and the world around them can be described as a dialogue, an interplay of question and answer. Science develops between the questions and the answers. For example, planning may involve thinking about 'What might happen if...?', considering evidence may include making comparisons – 'Which was the fastest?' – or providing explanations – 'What happened when...?'

Experienced learners may not be aware of using a question and answer strategy to aid thinking and learning – many questions are internalised and involve the use of complex language – but for pupils with learning difficulties this is a difficult process (Ritchie 2001, Bell 2002). While some may respond appropriately to recall and labelling questions (for example 'Look – what is it?', 'What did we see in the woods?', 'What's the name of the bone that protects your head?') most pupils find higher-order questions (for example, those concerned with reasoning, analysis and evaluation) far more difficult to use and to understand. For many pupils these skills will have to be taught, with adults and peers demonstrating questioning strategies explicitly, out loud, across a range of planned experiences and activities.

Thinking about the mechanical car

While playing with a mechanical car dialogue is modelled by a member of the staff team:

> How can I move the car?
> I'll try this way.
> Oh! dear it didn't move.
> What can I do this time?
> It moves if I pull it backwards first and then let go.
> Will it move along the carpet?
> Yes, but not very quickly.
> Why?
> Because the carpet is soft and the floor is hard.

Teachers should remain aware of the need to challenge pupils in this way and to provide them with regular opportunities to practise these techniques. For some pupils, a prompt sheet in the form of a 'lesson plan' may help (see Figure 2.1). By providing a framework of questions, with symbols where necessary, pupils are supported in taking responsibility for their own learning by independently organising, completing and evaluating the task. Initially they can read the prompts out loud, then silently as their skills progress, before rejecting the sheet completely in favour of independent learning and recording.

Other pupils will benefit from more intensive support where, at each stage, they are encouraged to record their decisions using pictures, symbols or text. Often completed alongside an adult or within a mixed ability group, these worksheets provide opportunities for individual pupils to learn about questioning through modelling and/or being offered just the right amount of assistance to help make the task an enjoyable experience (see Figures 2.2 and 2.3).

- What do I need?

- What am I trying to find out?

- What do I do next?

- How do I do it?

- What happened?

- Could I make it work better?

- Did I like/dislike this activity?

Figure 2.1 Prompt sheet to support progress towards independent learning

The importance of play

It is our belief that through play pupils can actively and meaningfully gain access to a wide range of scientific activities. Play that is well planned and pleasurable helps children to think, to increase their understanding and to improve their language competence. It allows children to be curious and creative, to explore and investigate materials, to experiment and to draw and test their conclusions. To this end it is a powerful teaching tool yet one favoured mainly for younger pupils, the assumption being that play is less relevant beyond the age of five (Wood and Attfield 1996) and sadly, inappropriate for pupils in secondary classes in both mainstream and specialist settings.

The fact that play as a teaching approach is used only with younger pupils is a tragedy and a puzzle. Few people outgrow the need for unrestrained experimentation or play. How many adults will pick up a magnifying glass and examine the pores of their skin, make a paper boat and 'race' it down the river or fly a kite? Educationalists know that children learn through play yet they lose sight of this in particular when it comes to pupils with learning difficulties to the extent that 'work' and 'play' are totally separate (Sherratt and Peter 2002). Play is also a victim of contentious issues, for example, age-appropriateness (Coupe O'Kane and Goldbart 1996, Farrell 1997) and the requirement to collect evidence of learning for assessment and target setting purposes (Wood and Bennett 1997, QCA/DfEE 2001d).

Age-appropriateness

From the arguments in favour to those strongly against, the issue of age-appropriateness produces extreme views. Burrows (2000) states that age-appropriateness should be a tool to expand opportunities while respecting choices. We would support this view but also believe that promoting a sense of playfulness and fun – no matter how childlike – will encourage and motivate active involvement with others and their environment. What is crucial is that practitioners respect individuality. In support of this Lacey (2001: 126) points out that: 'age-appropriateness is more connected with the way in which one treats and values people with learning difficulties. It has very little to do with taking teddy bears and children's songs away from them.'

According to Nind and Hewett (1994), we vary enormously in our individual abilities to be playful and in our attitudes to play but it is still a deeply enjoyable experience for

Investigating

What   I   will   do.

What   I   need.

Who   will   help   me?

Figure 2.2 Prompt sheet to support aspects of planning for an investigation

© Claire Marvin and Chris Stokoe (2003) *Access to Science*, David Fulton Publishers.

Investigating

What   I   did.

What   I   learned.

What   I   liked.

Figure 2.3 Prompt sheet to support aspects of reviewing an activity

many and it is our belief that this approach to learning should not be denied pupils with learning difficulties whatever their age and ability.

Science and play

Science is a versatile subject. It can be a springboard for playful activities that are novel and creative, that stimulate pupils' interests, introduce choice making and provide a motivating context for learning. A great deal of sound scientific understanding can be engendered through purposeful play (Figure 2.4) but to structure appropriate experiences requires skilful teaching.

Figure 2.4 Scientific understanding can be engendered through purposeful play

Practitioners need to 'play' with science again, to be encouraging and imaginative, to introduce opportunities for interesting discoveries and results. The way that pupils respond to the opportunities on offer will depend largely on the attitudes and strategies adopted by the staff team (Fisher 1990). Play is fun and having fun can be scientific. What is more captivating? To sit in a whole-class group and watch an adult make an electric circuit from prepared resources – Blue Peter-style, at the front of the class – or to explore and investigate the components in pairs. Which of the following approaches more effectively holds attention and encourages the development and use of thinking skills? To answer whole-class questions related to the teacher demonstration or to learn actively by operating the switch, achieving an effect and experiencing the immediate reaction of friends?

It is important that practitioners develop a proactive approach towards recognising and taking full advantage of every playful event and its scientific potential. Many activities that take place in schools do so already in a scientific context. This may remain unacknowledged and can be overlooked as incidental to other learning (NCC 1992b, Howe 1992). For pupils in all key stages valuable experiences and opportunities exist in such play contexts as:

- water and sand exploration
- clay and dough exploration
- wheeled, battery-operated and clockwork toys
- drama and role-play corners, for example, the garage, the office, the vets' surgery, the pet shop, the disco, the dentist's, the mini-beast habitat, the jungle
- construction equipment, for example, Lego, Duplo, Meccano, Airfix
- playing musical instruments
- small-world imaginative toys such as animals and dolls
- gadgets, for example, mobile phones, hand-held games, walkie-talkies
- computers and hi-tech toys set up for free use
- outdoor play with fixed equipment and small apparatus
- modelling with junk materials.

Often used in a playful context dough is a consistently undervalued resource – cooked dough, stretchy dough, salt dough, bread dough, commercially prepared Playdough, pastry, pizza dough (see Resources for recipes). It is familiar, motivating, versatile and age-appropriate. Although far from comprehensive Figure 2.5 helps readers to identify its scientific potential and Figure 2.6 shows pupils finding out how dough can be changed.

The importance of support

Pupils with learning difficulties lack experience of play for many reasons, for example, they may have an autistic spectrum disorder or a physical impairment. A lack of imagination and/or a shortened attention span, for example, may lead to underdeveloped or repetitive play skills, therefore exploration and investigation through play, often guided by a more experienced other, should be planned for and encouraged.

Adult support may take several forms, for example, sensitively considered modelling, prompting or parallel play that includes responses to or comments on the actions of the pupil (see 'Hussain' box on p. 26). In addition it is important to provide exciting and responsive resources to develop and sustain interest. Good learning, Vygotsky (1978) suggests, is that within the 'zone of proximal development'. This serves to acknowledge the difference between the actual developmental level of the pupil and the potential

---

Sc1 Scientific enquiry

In addition to the following suggestions all activities with dough promote the development, practice and consolidation of scientific enquiry skills.

Sc2 Materials and their properties

Grouping and classifying materials

– explore and investigate the material

- explore using all available senses or focus on one sense
- recognise the similarities and differences, for example, compare dough made with plain flour and dough made with self-raising flour or with wholemeal flour; compare cooked and uncooked dough
- discover its properties, for example, hard or soft, rough or smooth, flexible, rigid or brittle

Changing materials

– physically change the material

- explore the changes which can be made physically using hands/using tools, for example, twisting, stretching, bending, making shapes

– mix materials to produce new materials

- add water to flour
- add flour to water
- add oil to flour
- add too much or too little of a substance

– explore change in materials by heating, cooling, freezing

- recognise how reactions can be useful, for example, heating dough to make it edible!
- compare heated and unheated dough, frozen dough and dough at room temperature

Interest can be maintained and extended by:

- changing the colour – add oil and/or black food colouring
- adding paste
- using dough for printing or forming words
- making models and painting or varnishing dough to make jewellery, 3-D models, artefacts and ornaments
- providing junk materials and accessories, for example, glitter, feathers, shells, twigs.

Figure 2.5 Playing with dough – the scientific potential

level which can be reached with the 'scaffold' of an experienced adult or peer. The gap between the two – the zone of proximal development – is skilfully bridged with the support of the adult or peer who helps the pupil to construct new understandings within their zone.

The role of the staff team in supporting pupils appropriately in playful experiences and activities is clearly significant. Bruner (1972) demonstrated the importance of this with his theory of flexibility of thought – an aspect of thinking crucial to effective learning (see below) yet difficult for pupils with learning difficulties to achieve. Appropriate play and playful activities provide for the development of this process by offering opportunities to try out possibilities, to put different elements of a situation together in various ways and to persevere with the solving of problems. By allowing time for pupils to play with objects and materials, to explore them intimately and to try out possibilities they begin to take control of their environment and their learning (Figure 2.8). The opportunity to do that, or at least to have an effect, is a process worth working towards for all pupils (Coupe O'Kane and Smith 1994, Mittler 2001).

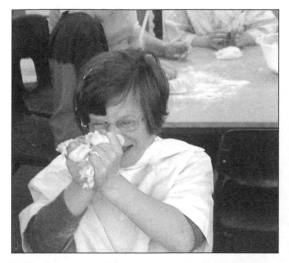

2.6a by squashing

2.6b by adding water

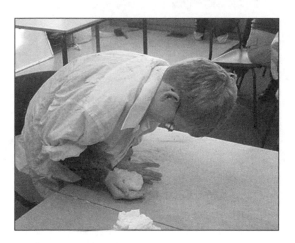

2.6c by patting

Figure 2.6 Finding out how dough can be changed

Supporting informal play – flexibility of thought theory

Bruner, in demonstrating his theory of flexibility of thought, planned a series of experiments where children were asked to solve practical problems. These activities illustrated the importance of allowing time for children to play with objects, to explore them intimately – making use of all the senses – and to try out possibilities. One group of children were given the opportunity to play with the objects involved, while the other group was 'taught' how to use them in ways which would help solve the problem. Consistently the 'play' group outperformed the 'taught' group when they were then left alone to tackle the problem. The children who had the experience of playing with the materials were more inventive in devising strategies to solve the problem, they persevered longer when their initial attempts failed and so were not surprisingly more successful in their attempts to solve the problem.

(Sylva *et al.* 1974)

Hussain

Hussain is a Year 5 pupil in a mixed-ability class in a special school. Alongside his peers he is exploring rocks and minerals during an introductory lesson about materials and their properties. He picks out the shiny specimens and moves them in the light, trying to get them to sparkle. Each pupil has a magnifying glass but despite his best efforts Hussain fails to understand how his friends are using this tool. Lorraine, the teaching assistant, notices his interest and his frustration. She sits close by and models the use of the magnifying glass while making encouraging comments, 'I can see this one shine', 'look at the big crystals' (Figure 2.7). Subsequently Hussain and Lorraine take turns to inspect the rocks. He is completely fascinated by the magnifying glass and its effect. Lorraine reinforces Hussain's involvement by attracting the attention of his peers to share the experience. His skills improve to the extent that in the following lesson he requires very little support to use the magnifying glass appropriately.

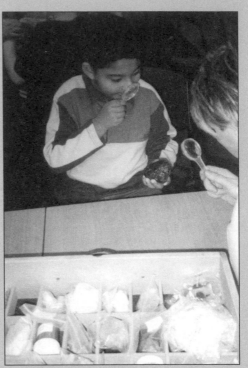

Figure 2.7 Sensitively considered modelling assists the learning process

It is our belief that Bruner's findings present further important implications for how teachers can most effectively provide the right kind of environment for pupils to learn, which for the purposes of this book relates to science and scientific contexts. Briefly they should be wary of presenting formal tasks too soon. While tightly structured activities may provide rich experiences for learning this is enhanced if pupils are first allowed to play freely with the materials provided. More particularly, if resources are unusual or new to the group, pupils will need time, supported or unsupported, to investigate and to relate their discoveries to known experiences and behaviours. For example, playing in the mud or in puddles, collecting natural resources that feel or move in an attractive way, investigating a new construction kit, observing a pet or riding a skateboard. Following this period of unrestrained exploration more structured tasks and learning outcomes can be introduced. The balance to be struck will depend on the range of needs, interests, past achievements and experiences of the pupils.

So why play? Why not? Play opens a window into pupils' minds and can reveal how they are emerging as learners and thinkers. When opportunities for unexpected discovery are combined with planned scientific activities and to this is added the curiosity of most pupils at whatever stage of cognitive, social and emotional development it is not difficult to arouse excitement and interest so that science lessons become motivating and fun. In the words of Jordan and Libby (1997: 29) 'play both

Figure 2.8 Exploratory play with objects and materials

develops in itself and is essential to other development. It is not the obverse of work: it is the work of children, who must discover the world through activity on it with others.'

Other approaches

There are two further approaches to learning and teaching that we believe deserve description in this chapter although the list is far from comprehensive. In our experience both are effective tools for stimulating curiosity and encouraging active learning.

Interactive displays or science corners

These offer opportunities for exploration and discovery through active use of available senses. Simple to organise they provide incidental moments to try things out, to 'see what happens if . . . ' and to have a go, either independently or with the support of an adult who, as stated previously, can model questions, 'scaffold' discovery and encourage recording (see Figure 2.9).

A 'colour' corner may contain:

- assorted sizes of coloured paper – cellophane, reflective, hologram, tissue
- junk materials, for example, cardboard tubes and sticky tape
- torches
- a kaleidoscope
- reflective and non-reflective materials
- unwanted CD-ROMs and their cases (the CD-ROMs reflect colours and can be decorated; the empty cases can be filled with coloured paper and hung as mobiles)
- lava lamp, manageable fibre-optic equipment, disco lights and switch access
- transparent or coloured pots and shakers with noisy or coloured contents
- a box of attractive resources to sort and group, for example, hair accessories, marbles, coloured bottles, ribbons, glittery socks
- worksheets to be completed with support
- 'choose to investigate' boxes.

'Choose to investigate' boxes

Teachers may, according to the experiences and capabilities of individual or groups of pupils, decide that 'choose to investigate' boxes are only accessed with help. In this case each pack has a large 'help' symbol on the lid supported by the words 'first ask for help'. The boxes contain activities that require adult or peer support, for example, colour mixing using a salad spinner and paint or food colouring (!), playing with a Spirograph, blow painting using straws, marbling activities, exploring prisms.

Figure 2.9 The colour corner

Sabotage

Sabotage lends itself particularly well to the development of skills involved in scientific enquiry and problem solving. Put simply, an element of a class routine, the familiar classroom environment or a popular activity is 'sabotaged' perhaps in a ridiculous or outrageous manner. In this way a touch of unpredictability, surprise and fun is introduced as well as providing serious opportunities to practise and develop the skills of scientific enquiry. For example remove the batteries from a torch, put holes in waterproof materials or too much water in the cake recipe.

Summary

Within the context of science a variety of teaching approaches are used. In choosing the most effective methods practitioners use their professional judgement to take into account the needs, abilities and preferences of individual and groups of pupils in addition to the intended learning outcomes of the planned experiences and activities and the resources available.

While science lends itself to investigative ways of working, aspects of this method – for example, questioning and reasoning – can be difficult for pupils with learning difficulties. As a result pupils require sensitive support and encouragement from a committed staff team who can make learning fun.

CHAPTER THREE

The practical planning materials – how to use them

This chapter supports and describes the practical materials presented in Chapters 5–9. It exemplifies a planning framework for the implementation of curriculum subjects – in this case science – in a school for pupils with severe and profound and multiple learning difficulties. Equally the format could be used or adapted for any school or educational setting.

The framework comprises:

- an overview of the skills and procedures that underpin scientific investigations (Sc1) across the key stages and examples of how they link to the content of science set out in Sc2–4 (see Chapter 5)
- suggestions for appropriate learning at each key stage
- long-term planning (not included in the practical materials)
- medium-term planning – subject leader
- medium-term planning – class teacher
- short-term planning
- resources.

Suggestions for appropriate learning

Based on the QCA/DfEE guidelines (2001a) the introduction to each chapter describes appropriate learning for pupils with diverse needs at each key stage. It is not meant to be prescriptive nor self-contained. Effective planning includes experiences and learning opportunities based on the needs, interests, past experiences and achievements of all pupils. For this reason practitioners may find relevant content in different key stages described in further chapters. In addition the *Early Learning Goals* (QCA/DfEE 1999), accreditation schemes (for example, ASDAN) and other local and national initiatives should also be consulted (see Resources). This flexible approach to planning builds on the principles of inclusion set out in the National Curriculum (DfEE/QCA 1999b) and supports the *Key Stage 3 National Strategy* framework for teaching science (DfES 2002a) that states, once an area for study has been chosen teachers should track back the scientific ideas to a level appropriate for the pupils and then plan to present the material in a context well-suited to the age group.

While progression in curriculum content can usually be demonstrated from key stage to key stage through skill development and acquisition of knowledge and understanding, progress for some pupils will be very slow. For this reason it may be necessary to provide frequent repetitions of the same experience; a particular learning opportunity may remain relevant and important for pupils for months or years. To this end some aspects of content may remain the same. Progression from key stage to key stage may be more concerned with generalising and extending previous learning to different environments, resources and levels of support than movement up a hierarchical ladder of skills and knowledge (see Chapter 10).

Long-term planning

Most practitioners are familiar with the process of planning in the long term for subjects in the curriculum. The QCA/DfEE (2001b: 14) guidelines suggest that long-term plans:

- indicate how content and skills in each key stage and programme of study are covered
- identify when it is appropriate to use blocked units and continuing units
- show links between subjects
- build in progression, consolidation and diversification for pupils across units.

In any individual school setting the process of planning at this stage can be complex. It involves extensive and ongoing discussion, coordination, monitoring and evaluation (Byers and Rose 1996). Within science, as for every subject, decisions will be influenced by pupils' individual needs in each age group, for example, at Key Stage 4, in preparation for increased independence outside and beyond school, a stand-alone module of work on 'electricity and its uses' may be planned, while the theme of 'growing-up' may represent a recurring unit of work with similar and additional content that pupils access regularly in age-appropriate contexts.

Long-term planning provides an invaluable whole-school perspective for each subject. It is very individual – its form, in part, depending on the size of the school it serves. The document is ongoing and subject to review. It may, for example, comprise units of work to be accessed over a number of years, or perhaps, a modular two-year rolling programme. For these reasons this highly individual process is not exemplified in this book, but the themes for the units of work are taken from a long-term curriculum map in a school for pupils with learning difficulties where science often forms the main focus to which other subjects are linked.

Science weeks

It is at this stage in the planning process that 'periods of intensive study' (QCA/DfEE 2001b: 13) can be added to the long-term curriculum map. These may include science weeks in which pupils of a particular age or key stage are 'immersed' in a scientific theme. Especially at Key Stage 4, in line with the changing needs of the pupils, the balance of curriculum content may alter, making a science week an opportunity to concentrate on scientific experiences and activities for a limited period of time as an alternative to regular timetabled lessons.

In our experience the hard work associated with planning for a science week is well worth the effort. It represents a change in routine – an important and necessary experience for some pupils – an opportunity to 'play with science' and to practise scientific and cross-curricular skills. With careful planning, it is an ideal way to present activities with dramatic results. Using all of their available senses pupils can explore unusual resources, show responses to special effects and participate in imaginative role play. They take risks, make choices and 'see what happens if . . .' – all effective ways of stimulating interest and excitement, and all offering access to, and opportunities for, learning that is pleasurable and fun (Figure 3.1).

Subject leader's medium-term planning

Compiled by the subject leader alone, or in collaboration with colleagues, the medium-term planning advice supports teachers in planning termly or half-termly units of work

Figure 3.1 Pupils taking part in science week

for individual classes or groups of pupils. The advice builds on and conforms to the information given on the long-term map and indicates how the work relates to the National Curriculum programmes of study. Following closely the description in the QCA/DfEE (2001b) guidelines the format provides:

- intended learning outcomes
- information on teaching activities and experiences
- descriptions of pupil behaviours offered as a means of assessing potential outcomes.

Differentiation

To aid differentiation two pages of teaching ideas are presented for each unit of work. They are:

- the foundation stage, and
- the access and extension stage.

The separation is linked to the continuum of need and aids teachers in planning appropriate experiences and activities for individual and groups of pupils. The teaching ideas, though separate, are seen as complementary. When used alongside each other to aid planning, activities and learning outcomes will, for example, promote access, participation and achievement for pupils with profound and multiple learning difficulties and also challenge those who may be assessed as reaching Level 1 of the National Curriculum.

Since the performance descriptions (P levels) published in the QCA/DfEE (2001a) guidelines seek to provide a common structure and language for recognising progress and attainment in pupils working below Level 1 of the National Curriculum, the stages of development used for differentiation purposes in this book can best be described as follows:

- foundation stage   – pupils working within P1–3(ii)
- access stage   – pupils working within P4–7
- extension stage   – pupils working within P8–towards Level 2 of the National Curriculum although it is not expected that pupils will attain this level across all areas of the science curriculum.

Explanation of format

Intended learning outcomes

This area of the planning advice describes the intended learning outcomes for individual or groups of pupils for the whole unit of work. It is implicit, at this stage, that practitioners bear in mind additional learning possibilities, for example, key skill areas (Chapter 1), and individual pupil targets embedded in pupils' individual education plans (IEPs).

Key words are provided for guidance. It is expected that practitioners will modify and extend these suggestions, for example, to include symbols or additional words, according to the needs of their pupils.

Teaching activities and experiences

In no particular hierarchical order these activities and experiences form the basis for the class teacher's planning for termly or half-termly units of work (see below).

Assessment prompts

This area of the planning advice relates to the intended learning outcomes and suggests responses and achievements that may be observed by members of a staff team and recorded as evidence of learning. To promote consistency with recently published curriculum materials (Dorchester Curriculum Group 2002, Cambridgeshire Cluster Group Project 2001, Turner 2002) and in accordance with the expectations of practitioners, the assessment prompts correspond to the P levels (QCA/DfEE 2001a). This is intended to help teachers make best-fit summative judgements about pupils' experiences and achievements over a period of time. In turn these decisions inform target setting and reporting.

Class teacher's medium-term planning

By selecting experiences and activities appropriate to an individual class or group of pupils from those suggested in the subject leader's medium-term planning advice, the class teacher may complete a detailed planning sheet for a series of lessons that constitute termly or half-termly units of work. Examples of these (one per key stage) are included in the practical materials which follow (see Chapters 6–9).

The class teacher's medium-term planning document is used to inform the teacher's short-term planning (if applicable). It should be viewed as an *aide-mémoire*, open to change and repetition according to the responses, participation and achievements of the pupils. Exemplified in Chapters 6–9 the planning sheets for this stage represent *one* format. Practitioners can adopt this or modify it to suit the requirements of their individual setting.

Completing the class teacher's planning document

The information in this section, although neither comprehensive nor prescriptive, is intended to highlight the uses of the class teacher's medium-term planning document and support practitioners in completing this stage of the planning process.

The class teacher's medium-term planning may:

- define the purpose of each lesson and its relationship to the other lessons in the unit of work, to aid continuity and progression for individual or groups of pupils
- indicate relevant and differentiated experiences and activities to be undertaken week by week
- create opportunities for assessment as an integral part of teaching and learning
- provide cross-curricular links where knowledge or skills developed through other subjects can be put to practical use or reinforced in this context
- indicate resources needed.

Specific areas to consider are set out below.

Equality of access

Equality of access should be demonstrated for all pupils, for example, those with profound and multiple learning difficulties or autistic spectrum disorder; those at the foundation, access or extension stage.

Enquiry skills

The skills associated with *Scientific enquiry* (Sc1) are taught through contexts taken from the content areas of science (Sc2–4) set out in the programme of study. Planning may reflect this either at this level or in short-term plans or both. Specific aspects of Sc1 may be selected as a focus for development.

Differentiation

Differentiation is an important aspect of this planning stage. Depending on the curriculum aims and the group of pupils involved, it may entail considering a variety of characteristics, for example: age, learning style, interests, needs, experiences and previous achievements; interests and skills within the staff team. Tasks for foundation, access and extension stage pupils may be separate, resources different and opportunities for recording differentiated.

Progression

Consider the progressive framework for the lesson from week to week. For example, early sessions (perhaps lessons 1 and 2) may include introductions to key words, new songs or rhymes and possibly new subject knowledge; later lessons may involve pupils in paired work and opportunities to take greater responsibility for their own learning.

Assessment

It is important to be clear about why assessment is taking place and what is being assessed. For example, as a result of observations of pupils' progress a teacher may decide to repeat or change a lesson, having concluded that, in terms of pupil engagement, it was successful but the pupils struggled with the concepts introduced.

Set aside time for summative assessment at the end of a unit of work to gather evidence for internal monitoring and review in addition to statutory testing, reporting and target setting.

Short-term planning

The short-term plans in this book – one per key stage – exemplify single science-focused sessions, each being part of a series of lessons outlined in the class teacher's planning for the unit of work (see above). They support teaching and learning on a lesson-by-lesson basis and usually include:

- well differentiated learning outcomes, experiences and activities drawn from the subject leader's and/or class teacher's planning
- targets from IEPs, usually set in terms of specific skills. These can be acquired, developed, practised and extended using science as a context for learning
- teaching methods
- pupil groupings and organisational issues, for example resources required.

In acknowledgement of excessive teacher work load individual schools are making efforts to reduce the quantity of paperwork expected from teachers in any particular week, term or year. The way in which medium- and short-term planning is seen as complementary greatly contributes to efficient practice. To this end the majority of successful primary schools (Ofsted 2002) adopt one of the following:

- medium-term planning in simple outline but with short-term plans written in detail
- medium-term planning written in detail but with short-term planning in simple outline.

In order to provide support for either structure both medium- and short-term plans are exemplified in detail in this book (see Chapters 6–9). It is for individual schools to determine and justify their approach to this issue and to ensure a balance between clarity of planning and the principles of good classroom practice.

Resources

Resource suggestions, for example, new songs from old favourites, that accompany specific planning advice complete each chapter. A general resources section can be found at the end of the book.

Summary

The planning framework described in this chapter is exemplified in the practical materials that follow. The exemplars should not be taken as definite but as guidance for practitioners to use as a catalyst for the development of their own ideas. They present one way of formatting the medium- and short-term planning process through which practitioners can offer equality of access to science-focused experiences and activities for pupils with learning difficulties.

CHAPTER FOUR

The practical planning materials – what they are

The practical materials that follow in Chapters 5–9 provide support and ideas for the effective planning and implementation of well-differentiated science-focused activities at each key stage. In addition to being used as a teaching resource it is hoped they will stimulate and support practitioners to reflect on their practice and to participate in curriculum development within increasingly inclusive educational settings.

The materials are drawn directly from practice. They have been developed, trialled, monitored and reviewed by the authors in a school for pupils with severe and profound and multiple learning difficulties. They are equally useful to those practitioners who teach pupils with significant special educational needs in a range of schools.

Chapter 5 provides an overview of *Scientific enquiry* (Sc1) – the continuous element of the science curriculum – and describes possible learning outcomes from which teachers can select appropriately for individual or groups of pupils. It also exemplifies links to the content of science (Sc2–4).

The planning materials for Key Stages 1–3 in Chapters 6 to 8 exemplify the four areas of science that pupils study. As suggested in the National Curriculum (DfEE/QCA 1999a), *Scientific enquiry* is taught through contexts taken from the sections on *Life processes and living things*, *Materials and their properties* and *Physical processes.* The number of plans correspond to the number of years pupils normally spend in each key stage – one unit of work is exemplified for each year. At Key Stage 4 the curriculum for pupils with severe and profound and multiple learning difficulties often diversifies and nationally accredited schemes, for example ASDAN and ALL (see Resources), or individual school programmes of study, are followed. To this end, two units of work are included for Key Stage 4 in Chapter 9. It is hoped that these will support and extend the contribution to learning made by certified schemes and national qualifications.

Content

Each chapter of practical materials is self-contained, but every plan and activity can be adopted or adapted according to the varied individual needs, interests, past experiences and achievements of all pupils in every age group. While Chapter 5 provides an overview of *Scientific enquiry* (Sc1), Chapters 6–9 present a common framework – one chapter per key stage as follows:

- suggestions for appropriate learning
- subject leader's medium-term planning advice
- class teacher's medium-term planning
- short-term planning
- resources, including songs and rhymes.

Photocopiable planning sheet formats are included in the Resources at the end of the book.

Units of work

Chapter 6	Key Stage 1		Page
		• Push and pull toys	56
		• Growing: green plants	60
		• Freezing and melting	64
Chapter 7	Key Stage 2		
		• Mini-beasts	78
		• Skeletons	82
		• Electricity	86
		• Washing and drying	90
Chapter 8	Key Stage 3		
		• Metals, non-metals and magnetism	106
		• Light and dark, the Earth and beyond	110
		• Nutrition and dental care	114
Chapter 9	Key Stage 4		
		• Horticulture	126
		• Sound	130

CHAPTER FIVE

Practical materials – scientific enquiry

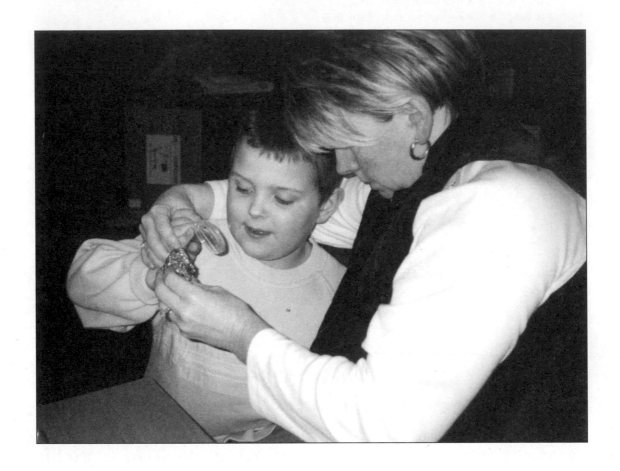

Through the appropriate development and use of the skills and attitudes set out in the *Scientific enquiry* (Sc1) section of the National Curriculum programme of study for science (DfEE/QCA 1999a) pupils may arrive at a better understanding of ideas about the physical and natural world. These skills and attitudes underpin success in all exploratory and investigative activities that are central to pupils' experiences in science and also form part of the core key and thinking skills that improve learning across subjects and in life outside and beyond school (see Chapter 1). For teachers they provide a fundamental starting point for planning effective science-focused learning experiences linked to the acquisition of subject-specific knowledge and understanding.

Within the programme of study for science, *Scientific enquiry* (Sc1) is divided into two parts:

1. Ideas and evidence in science

2. Investigative skills.

The *Ideas and evidence in science* section introduces the learner to the importance of:

- the generation of questions to be tested and developed through the process of gathering evidence – the basis for scientific enquiry
- the evaluation of evidence and consideration of how the results link to and impact on everyday lives.

The *Investigative skills* section sets out the particular skills required to carry out a full investigation under the following headings:

- planning
- obtaining and presenting evidence
- considering evidence and evaluating.

Put simply these skills constitute the before, during and after stages of an enquiry and although certain aspects of the process may be emphasised in order to support the development of particular skills, in practice they are interrelated and the whole resembles a cycle of investigation as described in Figure 5.1.

Aim

Through a broad range of scientific experiences and activities *Scientific enquiry* (Sc1), therefore, offers all pupils opportunities to build on their existing skills and attitudes to:

- develop and extend key skills for learning
- develop and extend thinking
- plan and carry out investigations
- obtain and present findings
- evaluate evidence
- link scientific knowledge and understanding to everyday events.

Practical activities

Practical activities offer first-hand concrete experiences that provide an effective route to learning. Those most appropriate for the development and use of scientific skills and procedures are:

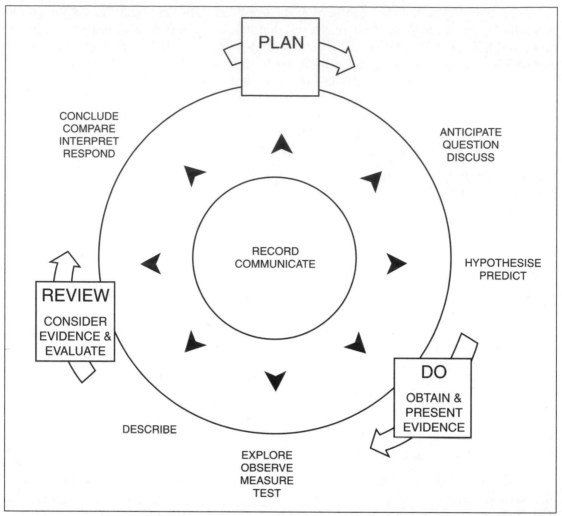

Figure 5.1 Scientific enquiry – the cycle of investigation skills (adapted from Jones and Skelton 1993, Hollins and Whitby 2001)

- exploration
- classification
- investigation.

While individual in nature these activities are not mutually exclusive. Teachers may plan to incorporate all of them into one lesson or a series of lessons depending on the aims of the unit of work and the needs, interests, past experiences and achievements of the pupils.

Exploration enables pupils to access information about themselves and the world around them. It is a vital part of the learning process. So that interest and curiosity may be aroused and sustained every pupil should have regular opportunities to develop and use their available senses and to make discoveries through first-hand sensory experiences (Figure 5.2). Following on from this they may, independently or with 'enabling' support, try out further actions that link to exciting consequences. In turn, these may lead to the development of skills associated with planning a simple investigation.

Figure 5.2 The delight and wonder of exploration – Jenny holding a vibrating top

Jamie

Jamie likes to be close to people. He responds by smiling, vocalising and turning his head. He particularly likes glittering objects. The teaching assistant, Sarah, wants to encourage him, by using his available senses, to explore and interact with his immediate surroundings. She wears shiny things, for example, a wig, hat, earrings, spectacles, while sitting close to him in a quiet room. With the lights correctly adjusted Jamie is attracted briefly to the shimmering objects. He glances towards them, smiles and slightly raises his arm. Sarah is ready to interpret this action as a reach towards her. She responds with dramatic effect – the shiny hat falls to the floor, Sarah pulls a face and blows a very loud raspberry. Jamie renews his attention, this time to her face.

Classification activities can be structured in different ways and at different levels. They encourage pupils to think, question and think again. Pupils begin by making simple collections of natural materials or familiar objects, for example, leaves, light sources, noise makers. This may lead to sorting and grouping activities involving the recognition of similarities and differences, for example, separating white vegetables from the rest, shiny from dull materials, pupils with dark hair from those with light-coloured hair, or to the recording of evidence during an investigation, for example, those materials that are good insulators or water resistant.

Investigation has three phases – planning, doing and reviewing – and while the emphasis may vary, all three parts are present in most investigations. Developing the ability to independently plan and conduct a fair test and subsequently to review and reflect on the evidence takes time and practice and, in our experience, is usually beyond the ability of pupils with learning difficulties. However the cycle of skills involved (see Figure 5.1) forms a strategy for planning interesting learning opportunities and, with appropriate support and skilful modelling, makes it possible to include pupils in all aspects of the enquiry. In addition, open-ended investigations allow for learning at a variety of levels – in a lesson about physical changes to materials, for example, one pupil may show interest in the changes that occur while another may question why they take place. Figures 5.3 to 5.6 show pupils involved in different phases of various investigations.

Figure 5.3 Year 10 pupils have planned an investigation on growing plants and visit the garden centre

Figure 5.4 Lauren observes the movement of a guinea pig

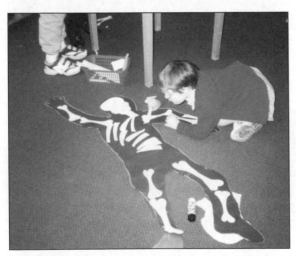

Figure 5.5 Julie records her work on skeletons

Figure 5.6 Susan uses a recording sheet to structure her work at the Water Park

Martin

Martin is a Year 6 pupil. He has severe learning difficulties and an autistic spectrum disorder exacerbated by cerebral palsy and a hearing impairment. As part of a science-focused activity on seeds and fruits he is offered an assortment of brightly-coloured produce to explore. Immediately engaged he 'plans' his activity by taking the tomato. Without a pause he squashes it and pulls it apart. Chuckling with delight he watches the pulp and seeds spill over his hands and shoot across the classroom. Martin is 'doing'! He explores the remnants until they are gone!

Eagerly he requests another and with increasingly sophisticated exploration skills he examines the shiny red skin, touching it gently with his index finger and turning the fruit round so it catches the light then he gives it back to the teacher with an expectant grunt. Martin watches with interest as she splits open the tomato and returns it to him (Figure 5.7). He licks, inspects and slowly destroys the flesh while, at the same time, observing the results of his actions. All too soon it is gone.

In a subsequent lesson Martin notices more tomatoes. He is very excited – rocking his chair, banging his tray and vocalising. He looks towards the selection of fruit and back to the teacher who offers him a choice once again. In anticipation of the fun to follow he takes the tomato. Martin is beginning to 'review' his experiences by demonstrating his preference and showing a consistent response.

The cycle of investigation begins again.

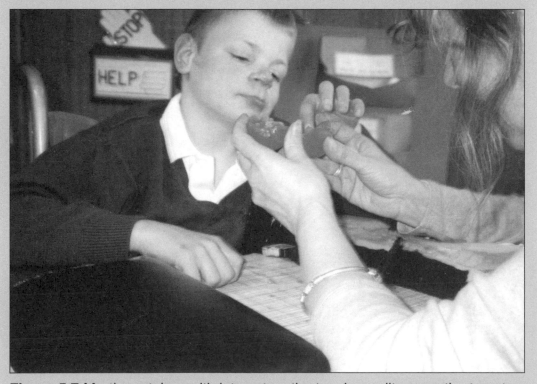

Figure 5.7 Martin watches with interest as the teacher splits open the tomato

Planning for scientific enquiry

Planning for and teaching the development of the skills, strategies and attitudes set out in the *Scientific enquiry* (Sc1) section of the programme of study for science is complex and demanding but, as previously stated, essential for effective learning in science and across the whole curriculum. Experiences and activities must be well differentiated and flexible according to the wide range of needs of individual and groups of pupils. For example, in a particular class or key stage some pupils may be developing fleeting responses to familiar objects and their effects while others are systematically observing materials and noting their similarities and differences. With each pupil bringing a unique starting point to the equation this places particularly high demands on practitioners. However, it is our view that despite these challenges all pupils can be included, at an appropriate level and with support, in all aspects of scientific enquiry.

Under the headings set out in the 'Investigative skills' section of *Scientific enquiry* (Sc1) – 'planning', 'obtaining and presenting evidence' and 'considering evidence and evaluating' – the remainder of this chapter sets out suggestions for appropriate learning outcomes for individual or groups of pupils and exemplifies links to the content of science set out in Sc2–4. The individual tables define aspects of the skills and attitudes of scientific enquiry to be developed and extended at each stage of development which, for the purposes of this book, are known as 'foundation' (Tables 5.1–5.3), 'access' (Tables 5.4–5.6) and 'extension' (Tables 5.7–5.9) (see Chapter 3). Boundaries between skills are artificial, fragmenting what is, in practice, a whole, but by examining them separately we believe that a common and clear notion of the parts that constitute the investigation process becomes evident. It is for individual teachers to establish the relevance of specific skill areas for their pupils and to plan appropriately – for example, by identifying smaller units of learning that can be gradually combined towards a whole investigation.

Table 5.1 Foundation stage – planning

Scientific enquiry skills	
FOUNDATION stage (P1–3)	

Aims

Through a broad range of scientific experiences and activities pupils will be given opportunities to build on their existing knowledge, skills, understanding and attitudes to:

- develop an awareness of and interest in themselves and their immediate surroundings and environment
- develop and use their senses to explore
- understand object permanence
- begin to understand that actions have consequences – cause and effect
- develop simple problem-solving skills
- take control of their immediate environment, for example, by communicating needs, preferences and dislikes

Planning	Examples in the context of Sc2–4
Independently or with support pupils may: - anticipate known actions and events and their outcomes in familiar learning contexts	- attending to a sound source before it is activated - leaning forward to look at a large colourful tractor positioned at the top of a ramp and becoming excited when told to 'wait for it, wait for it!' - vocalising when presented with a preferred, switch-operated toy or device - associating a routine song with the end of an activity

Table 5.2 Foundation stage – obtaining and presenting evidence

Scientific enquiry skills
FOUNDATION stage (P1–3)
Aims Through a broad range of scientific experiences and activities pupils will be given opportunities to build on their existing knowledge, skills, understanding and attitudes to: • develop an awareness of and interest in themselves and their immediate surroundings and environment • develop and use their senses to explore • understand object permanence • begin to understand that actions have consequences – cause and effect • develop simple problem-solving skills • take control of their immediate environment, for example, by communicating needs, preferences and dislikes

Obtaining and presenting evidence	Examples in the context of Sc2–4
Independently or with support pupils should: • use their available senses to explore a wide range of living things, materials and phenomena to gather sensory information	• tolerating the sound of percussion instruments or being touched with different textures • giving fleeting attention to the movement of disco lights in a darkened room • indiscriminately exploring a range of materials with strong tactile, visual and/or aural qualities • purposefully exploring during a visit to the local woods – scrunching leaves, squeezing damp soil and searching for favourite items
• respond to instructions that relate to health and safety issues	• reacting to gestures and/or large bold symbols and signs, for example, 'stop', 'hot'
Independently or with support pupils may: • begin to solve simple unstructured problems	• searching for items that are out of sight
• attend and show an interest in the results of their actions	• looking at the monitor after randomly hitting a computer keyboard to colour in outlines of flowering plants

Table 5.3 Foundation stage – considering evidence and evaluating

Scientific enquiry skills
FOUNDATION stage (P1–3)

Aims
Through a broad range of scientific experiences and activities pupils will be given opportunities to build on their existing knowledge, skills, understanding and attitudes to:

- develop an awareness of and interest in themselves and their immediate surroundings and environment
- develop and use their senses to explore
- understand object permanence
- begin to understand that actions have consequences – cause and effect
- develop simple problem-solving skills
- take control of their immediate environment, for example, by communicating needs, preferences and dislikes

Considering evidence and evaluating	Examples in the context of Sc2–4
Independently or with support pupils may:	
• respond intermittently to familiar resources or unusual effects	• showing fleeting interest in the movement of a remote controlled car
• use a preferred method of communication to respond consistently to, and comment on, familiar resources, experiences, actions or unusual effects	• vocalising and smiling when floating in water • relaxing while experiencing the sensations of swinging, revolving and rocking
• demonstrate preferences and dislikes for a wide range of living things, materials and phenomena	• rejecting the smell and taste of a selection of foods • reaching out to select a preferred light source from a limited selection
• begin to generalise skills in less familiar environments	• tipping containers to gain access to the contents, for example, natural or man-made materials, food shopping, light sources, battery-operated appliances

Table 5.4 Access stage – planning

Scientific enquiry skills	
ACCESS stage (P4–7)	

Aims

Through a broad range of scientific experiences and activities pupils will be given opportunities to build on their existing knowledge, skills, understanding and attitudes to:

- develop an awareness of and interest in themselves and their environment
- develop and use their senses to explore and investigate
- understand that actions have consequences – cause and effect
- develop problem-solving skills
- take control of their environment, for example, by communicating needs, preferences and dislikes
- participate in investigations that begin to link to ideas

Planning	Examples in the context of Sc2–4
Independently or with support pupils may:	
• in familiar and increasingly less familiar learning contexts understand that actions have consequences and that these are linked – cause and effect	• watching the end of a funnel and waiting for the water to pour out • pressing a switch to play a tune
• contribute to discussion about possible methods and materials for investigations and be involved in the selection and gathering of resources	• choosing different fabrics to stain and wash and knowing that water is needed for the test
• begin to make connections and predictions by drawing on previous experience	• predicting that an ice block will melt when left in the sun or in hot water • predicting which surfaces will be slippery
• know about and begin to use a range of simple secondary sources to gather information	• finding books about flowering plants in the school library

Table 5.5 Access stage – obtaining and presenting evidence

Scientific enquiry skills
ACCESS stage (P4–7)

Aims

Through a broad range of scientific experiences and activities pupils will be given opportunities to build on their existing knowledge, skills, understanding and attitudes to:

- develop an awareness of and interest in themselves and their environment
- develop and use their senses to explore and investigate
- understand that actions have consequences – cause and effect
- develop problem-solving skills
- take control of their environment, for example, by communicating needs, preferences and dislikes
- participate in investigations that link to ideas

Obtaining and presenting evidence	Examples in the context of Sc2–4
Independently or with support pupils should:	
• use their available senses to explore and investigate a wide range of living things, materials and phenomena at first through free play and then to begin to gather information systematically	• searching for tactile animal toys hidden in straw • observing the movement of tadpoles in the natural environment and/or in a glass tank • exploring different kinds of food
• respond to and follow instructions that relate to health and safety issues and begin to be aware of personal safety	• knowing to use heatproof gloves to remove dishes from an oven • knowing not to mouth seeds
Independently or with support pupils may:	
• develop and practise skills of observation and use simple methods of recording	• sorting small-world animals from people • sorting objects that sink from those that float; objects that are soft from those that are hard • finding 'one that's different' or 'one the same' in a collection of objects
• begin to recognise and use simple scientific equipment	• using a pond-dipping net or magnet
• answer simple questions that use familiar scientific language	• pointing to a pictorial image of a cat on request • saying if the item is 'hot' or 'cold'
• use a preferred method of communication and/or simple scientific language to describe experiences and evidence gathered	• using the words 'rough' and 'smooth' to describe the properties of sandpaper and cellophane • making a pictogram of basic light sources using photographs or symbols

Table 5.6 Access stage – considering evidence and evaluating

Scientific enquiry skills
ACCESS stage (P4–7)

Aims
Through a broad range of scientific experiences and activities pupils will be given opportunities to build on their existing knowledge, skills, understanding and attitudes to:

- develop an awareness of and interest in themselves and their environment
- develop and use their senses to explore and investigate
- develop problem-solving skills
- take control of their environment, for example, by communicating needs, preferences and dislikes
- participate in investigations that link to ideas
- comment on and begin to consider evidence

Considering evidence and evaluating	Examples in the context of Sc2–4
Independently or with support pupils may:	
• make choices, demonstrate preferences and dislikes	• showing preferences for some materials, for example, soft cottonwool rather than hard pebbles • choosing favourite sound makers • sampling and commenting on the results of a cooking session to investigate changes of state
• describe the results of investigations and make simple comparisons	• knowing that a thinner liquid is easier to pour than a thickened one
• use observations and non-standard measurements to begin to draw conclusions from evidence gathered	• concluding that light passes through some materials • concluding which bean plant grew the tallest and stayed green
• begin to suggest an explanation for what happened	• stating that the ice melted because it was in warm water
• begin to link scientific knowledge, skills and understanding to routine and/or familiar events	• knowing that some materials are more waterproof than others

Table 5.7 Extension stage – planning

Scientific enquiry skills
EXTENSION stage (P8 – towards Level 2 NC)

Aims

Through a broad range of scientific experiences and activities pupils will be given opportunities to build on their existing knowledge, skills, understanding and attitudes to:

- develop an awareness of and interest in themselves and their wider environment
- develop and use their senses to explore and investigate
- develop and use problem-solving skills
- take control of their wider environment, for example, by communicating needs and preferences
- participate in investigations that link to ideas

Planning	Examples in the context of Sc2–4
Independently or with support pupils may:	
• decide what methods to use and what evidence to collect to answer a scientific question	• communicating how a test may be planned to discover the strength of paper bags by exploring and collecting different paper, observing closely when water is added to the bags, predicting which papers will be the strongest
• begin to make appropriate comments related to planning a fair test	• suggesting planting the seeds in the *same* way by saying, 'put them all in the soil'
• answer scientific questions and begin to ask simple questions	• suggesting resources that can be collected to investigate light and its effectiveness in response to adult request • asking questions beginning mainly with 'why?'
• make generalisations and predictions by drawing on previous experience	• knowing that heat and heatproof vessels are needed to melt butter • recognising that a particular kitchen paper absorbs more spilt water than others
• select and gather appropriate resources	• gathering materials and resources to test for magnetic properties using their own simple criteria
• know about and use a range of secondary sources to gather information	• using an interactive computer program to find out about skeletons and body systems • viewing a video or using a CD-ROM simulation to find out about the rotation of the Earth and night and day

Table 5.8 Extension stage – obtaining and presenting evidence

Scientific enquiry skills
EXTENSION stage (P8 – towards Level 2 NC)

Aims

Through a broad range of scientific experiences and activities pupils will be given opportunities to build on their existing knowledge, skills, understanding and attitudes to:

- develop an awareness of and interest in themselves and their wider environment
- develop and use their senses to explore and investigate
- develop and use problem-solving skills
- take control of their wider environment, for example, by communicating needs and preferences
- participate in investigations that link to ideas

Obtaining and presenting evidence	Examples in the context of Sc2–4
Independently or with support pupils should:	
• use scientific enquiry skills, for example, observation, comparison to explore and investigate a wide range of living things, materials and phenomena and begin to gather information systematically	• sorting foliage according to colour or shape • observing and comparing the texture of untreated wooden logs and prepared wood • using non-standard measures, for example, Lego bricks or hands, to measure the height of a sunflower • observing and measuring the length of shadows at particular times during the day
• follow instructions that relate to health and safety issues and take action to control risks to themselves and others	• knowing that fruits and seeds can be poisonous and warning peers • knowing never to look directly at the sun
Independently or with support pupils may:	
• record what happens using a variety of methods	• completing a prepared record sheet using sticky picture symbols
• say what they are doing to make a test 'fair'	• using the *same* amount of Plasticine and/ or the *same* height of water in an investigation on the effects of shapes on water resistance
• use simple scientific equipment	• using a magnifying glass to examine rocks
• answer questions using appropriate scientific language	• using 'repel' or 'attract' to describe the behaviour of magnets and suggesting some magnetic items
• present and comment on results of investigations	• describing the properties of sandpaper and cellophane by using the words 'rough' and 'smooth' • using a software program to present data in different forms such as bar chart, pictures

Table 5.9 Extension stage – considering evidence and evaluating

Scientific enquiry skills
EXTENSION stage (P8 – towards Level 2 NC)
Aims Through a broad range of scientific experiences and activities pupils will be given opportunities to build on their existing knowledge, skills, understanding and attitudes to: • develop an awareness of and interest in themselves and their wider environment • develop and use their senses to explore and investigate • develop and use problem-solving skills • take control of their wider environment, for example, by communicating needs and preferences • participate in investigations that link to ideas • comment on and consider evidence

Considering evidence and evaluating	Examples in the context of Sc2–4
Independently or with support pupils may: • present evidence, explain the results and communicate the findings to others	• looking at a simple bar chart to decide which car travelled the fastest down the ramp and suggesting improvements for conducting the test the next time
• compare the results of investigations with original predictions	• looking at the results of baking a cake and discussing predictions from basic ingredients • discovering and commenting on the most effective way to dry a wet sheet
• begin to use evidence for a purpose, to link scientific knowledge, skills and understanding to everyday events and to generalise skills in new and unfamiliar situations	• knowing that thermos flasks keep food warm • knowing about effective stain removal methods • understanding that pushes and pulls can make things start moving, speed up, slow down or stop

CHAPTER SIX

Practical materials for Key Stage 1

Experiences and opportunities at Key Stage 1

The focus of teaching science at Key Stage 1 may be on giving pupils opportunities to:

- experience and explore their immediate surroundings through a broad range of sensory activities using familiar resources, and unfamiliar resources that have dramatic effects, for example, magnets, Soundbeam, alarm clock
- respond to and engage in playful, first-hand activities and investigations that raise awareness of and curiosity about themselves and their abilities to control their immediate environment.

Given these opportunities in science at Key Stage 1 the QCA/DfEE (2001a: 10) guidelines suggest that:

all pupils with learning difficulties (including those with the most profound disabilities)	build on their own experiences and on the exploration and investigation opportunities given in the foundation stage. They take part in scientific enquiry by exploring people, materials and other living things and respond to sensory experiences.
most pupils with learning difficulties (including those with severe difficulties in learning) who will develop further skills, knowledge and understanding in most aspects of the subject	become familiar with some scientific language. They are aware that their actions have consequences, *for example, personal cause and effect*, and that they can change materials. They collect evidence as part of scientific enquiry.
a few pupils with learning difficulties who will develop further aspects of knowledge, skills and understanding in the subject	record and communicate their ideas and data, *for example, using drawings, objects, symbols*, and begin to evaluate evidence. They may answer scientific questions and use scientific language.

Learning opportunities at Key Stage 1

Tables 6.1–6.6 are examples of a subject leader's medium-term plans for science-focused units of work at Key Stage 1 covered over a term or half a term. These are followed by Table 6.7, an example of a class teacher's planning sheet for a series of weekly lessons from a selected unit of work, and Table 6.8, a short-term plan exemplifying a single session from within the series.

Table 6.1 Example of a subject leader's medium-term planning – Key Stage 1, Foundation, Sc4 Push and pull toys

Subject Leader's Medium-term Planning

Key Stage: 1 Foundation	Subject: Science	PoS: Sc4 Push and pull toys	Curriculum links: PE	L-TP reference: Year 1 Spring 1
Intended learning outcomes	Activities		Assessment prompts	
Sc1: Scientific enquiry All pupils will encounter a range of scientific experiences and sensory resources linked to the programme of study (PoS). These opportunities will provide a context in which pupils learn to: • demonstrate emerging awareness **P1(ii)** • respond and show interest **P2(i)** • engage and explore indiscriminately **P2(ii)** • participate intentionally **P3(i)** • initiate involvement. **P3(ii)**	Introduce the PoS by exploring a variety of large and small push and pull toys. Use a large blanket or parachute, pull the pupils across the floor. Count before you move them to build anticipation. *PE link* Use a hammock, rocking chair or PE bench to push pupils and enable them to experience and anticipate the movement. Use large balloons, put rice inside before blowing up. Pin the balloon tied to a long string onto the ceiling. Sit the pupils in a circle and encourage them to reach out and push it to another peer. Encourage the pupils to track the balloon and anticipate their turn. Use helium-filled balloons with long strings. Encourage the pupils to let them go and then 'pull' them back. Reinforce the action by saying the word.		Pupils may: • demonstrate simple reflex responses and be resistant or passive to supported sensory activities. *Example*: blinking in response to being pushed in a hammock or being resistant to having gloves placed on their hands. **P1(i)** • focus their attention briefly on people, objects and events, and give intermittent reactions. *Example*: showing a fleeting awareness of a ball being rolled or focusing attention on an adult offering a resource. **P1(ii)** • accept and engage in supported exploration and reject or begin to show interest in new and unfamiliar activities and resources. *Example*: pulling the string of pull-along resource coactively or leaning to look at a moving toy. **P2(i)**	

Intended learning outcomes	Activities	Assessment prompts
	Use a selection of fabrics, e.g. textures, colours. Place them, one at a time, over your head, or that of the pupils. Encourage them to pull the cloth away, explore the fabrics and demonstrate preferences. Use fabrics to hide favourite noise-makers or cause and effect resources. Encourage pupils to pull the cloth away to find the resource.	• interact with people and begin to explore objects proactively; perform actions through supported trial and error and communicate preferences and dislikes. *Example:* pulling the cover from a familiar adult to reveal their face or gesturing towards a PE resource (e.g. physiotherapy ball) to indicate preference. **P2(ii)**
	Use large push- or pull-along resources. Sit the pupils on or in them and push or pull them across the playground or hall. Have races. Reinforce the words 'push' and 'pull' as you move the pupils. Build on anticipation work by cuing with: 'Ready, steady, go!' or '1 – 2 – 3'. *PE link* Use hats, gloves and socks: attach noise-makers or shiny objects. Encourage the pupils to pull on the hats and push their hands and feet into the gloves and socks or to pull these from you. Sit the pupils in front of a ramp or PE bench and encourage them to push wheeled resources or balls down it. Position another pupil at the end of the ramp to receive them.	• begin to show interest in and observe the results of their actions; choose to interact with people actively, and explore objects with less support. *Example:* pushing a ball towards a peer partner or familiar adult or pulling a cover off a toy with the intention of retrieving the object. **P3(i)** • explore objects independently for short periods and initiate interactions with people; demonstrate an emerging potential to solve simple problems and begin to anticipate the outcomes of activities. *Example:* anticipating a preferred movement (e.g. rocking in a hammock) by smiling, vocalising or body movement or reaching out to push a balloon hanging on a string.
Key words Push Pull Stop Fast Slow Go Slide	Use sensory toys that have a pull string (e.g. musical). Encourage the pupils to reach out and pull the string to make the resource work.	**P3(ii)**

Table 6.2 Example of a subject leader's medium-term planning – Key Stage 1, Access and Extension, Sc4 Push and pull toys

Subject Leader's Medium-term Planning

Key Stage: 1 Access & Extension	Subject: Science	PoS: Sc4 Push and pull toys	L-TP reference: Year 1 Spring 1
		Curriculum links: Maths, DT, PE	
Intended learning outcomes	**Activities**	**Assessment prompts**	
Sc1: Scientific enquiry To develop skills of scientific enquiry through activities which provide opportunities to: • anticipate and make choices • use senses to investigate materials and resources • observe, comment and measure • record and evaluate.	Use a variety of wind-up or mechanical toys. Make a track on the floor using coloured sticky tape to mark lanes. Have races; predict which toy will win. Make a scoreboard to record outcome. *Maths link* Use large push-pull resources. Pupils choose favourite then, matching 'push' toys with 'pull' toys, race with another peer. Pupils watching predict which toy will win, i.e. 'push' or 'pull'. Use scoreboard to record outcome. *Maths link*	Pupils may: • handle or observe resources with curiosity and demonstrate a general interest in their properties, features and functions; imitate familiar actions; know that certain actions cause predictable results. *Example:* pushing a car along a track or pressing the switch on a remote control toy. **P4** • focus on activities and anticipate actions; explore and group resources with support, and respond to simple scientific questions using their preferred method of communication.	
Sc4: Physical processes ***Access*** To recognise that toys can be moved by pushing and pulling them. To investigate ways of pushing and pulling a range of resources.	Look at magazines and catalogues to find pictures of push and pull toys. Cut them out and stick them onto a simple recording sheet. Go on a visit to the local park. Pupils take turns to push and pull one another on the swings and roundabouts. Take photographs or video for follow-up work.	*Example:* making sets of wheeled and non-wheeled toys or finding out which doors in school have to be pushed or pulled. **P5** • recognise features of living things and objects; begin to generalise and predict outcomes, and explore resources intentionally and appropriately and group them to simple given criteria. *Example:* predicting which toy will win a race or observing the behaviour of balloons when pushed under water and released. **P6**	

Intended learning outcomes	Activities	Assessment prompts
To use the words 'push' and 'pull' in a variety of contexts.	Fill a water tray or large bucket with water. Blow up balloons and encourage pupils to try to push the balloon under the water. What happens when they let go? Test other resistant resources, e.g. football, swimming floats.	• investigate resources purposefully and group them reliably; make observations and offer ideas using simple scientific language; begin to plan, record and evaluate their work with support. *Example*: recalling which actions they used when playing on park equipment (e.g. 'push' on swing) or knowing that a pull toy went further than a push toy. **P7**
Extension To investigate and test ways of moving larger resources (i.e. pushing or pulling).	Use a large PE ball and football. Have 'ball push' races and predict which one will win. Practise controlling a ball along a track. *PE link*	
	Use dressing-up box, encourage pupils to try on different clothes. Reinforce concept of pushing and pulling while dressing, e.g. 'pull it over your head'.	• make independent contributions to enquiries and answer simple reasoning questions; recognise similarities and differences in the features of living things and properties of objects consistently. *Example*: suggesting ways of moving a heavy object (e.g. pull with a rope) and making simple evaluations of the methods attempted. **P8**
	Use a heavy object, e.g. sandbag, give the pupils rope, string, chair, trolley. Work out how to move the object from one point to another. *DT link*	
	Go on a journey around school. Count how many doors have to be pushed or pulled. Make symbolic labels to stick on doors. Make a pictogram to record findings. *Maths link*	
Key words Push Pull Toy Move Slide Fast Slow Stop Go		Refer to the National Curriculum guidance for science assessment prompts beyond P8.

Table 6.3 Example of a subject leader's medium-term planning – Key Stage 1, Foundation, Sc2 Growing: green plants

Subject Leader's Medium-term Planning

Key Stage: 1 Foundation	Subject: Science	PoS: Sc2 Growing: green plants	Curriculum links: English, Art and design, Geography, Music, RE	L-TP reference: Year 2 Spring 2
Intended learning outcomes	Activities		Assessment prompts	
Sc1: Scientific enquiry All pupils will encounter a range of scientific experiences and sensory resources linked to the programme of study. These opportunities will provide a context in which pupils learn to: • demonstrate emerging awareness **P1(ii)** • respond and show interest **P2(i)** • engage and explore indiscriminately **P2(ii)** • participate intentionally **P3(i)** • initiate involvement. **P3(ii)**	Introduce the PoS by exploring a variety of plants and leaves within the school environment. Go on a visit to a local country park or woodland area. Experience sitting or walking under the trees. Explore the different textures. Make bark rubbings, collect broken bark. Photograph or video the visit for follow-up work. *Geography link* Explore the compost, water spray, containers, bulbs or seeds in tubs or pots (Figure 6.1). Make a 'flower' name label with each pupil, stick their photograph onto the centre of the flower, laminate and use to mark their pot. Make a 2- or 3-D reading tree, recording objects of reference, picture symbols, photographs that pupils recognise and respond to. New objects or pictures can be added as the pupils learn them. *English link* Make a class 'family tree'. Print with different materials and textures of paint, or use bark or textured fabric and materials. Add the pupils' photographs stuck onto leaves or flowers (this could be in chronological order).		Pupils may: • demonstrate simple reflex responses and be resistant or passive to supported sensory activities. *Example:* recoiling from the feel of compost or licking their lips in response to the smell or taste of marzipan. **P1(i)** • focus their attention briefly on people, objects and events, and give intermittent reactions. *Example:* giving fleeting attention to a brightly coloured flower or reacting to sunlight through the branches and leaves of a tree. **P1(ii)** • accept and engage in supported exploration and reject or begin to show interest in new and unfamiliar activities and resources. *Example:* exploring ready to roll icing by stretching or squeezing or rejecting the peppermint water using their preferred method of communication. **P2(i)**	

Intended learning outcomes	Activities	Assessment prompts
	Visit a florist's shop. Experience the sights and smells. Take photographs of the visit for follow-up work or personal records.	• interact with people and begin to explore objects proactively; perform actions through supported trial and error and communicate preferences and dislikes. *Example*: selecting a favourite resource from those used to illustrate rhymes and songs (e.g. silver bells in 'Mary, Mary') or screwing up tissue to make paper flower heads. **P2(ii)**
	Sing or listen to rhymes and songs relating to flowers, trees and plants, e.g. 'Ring o' ring o' roses', 'I had a little nut tree', 'Here we go round the mulberry bush'. Act out the rhymes using real objects as illustrations and for sensory exploration. *Music link*	
	Make an artificial bouquet of flowers for Mothers' Day, e.g. egg boxes to make daffodils, screwed up tissues to make carnations, painted art straws to form stems. Wrap the bouquets in cellophane and add coloured ribbons. *RE link*	• begin to show interest in and observe the results of their actions; choose to interact with people actively, and explore objects with less support. *Example*: actively exploring tree bark or pushing a bulb into a pot of compost. **P3(i)**
	Explore the sensory characteristics of rose, lavender and peppermint plants. Use rose, lavender or peppermint water to reinforce the smell. Encourage the pupils to make a choice and then use in a foot spa or in a water-play activity.	• explore objects independently for short periods and initiate interactions with people; demonstrate an emerging potential to solve simple problems and begin to anticipate the outcomes of activities. *Example*: choosing a pastry cutter to make flower shapes or anticipating being sprayed with a water spray. **P3(ii)**
	Make a tactile display of 'Mary, Mary, quite contrary'. Read the rhyme together and select different textures of materials and fabrics to produce the flowers and plants, e.g. silver bells. *Art and design link*	
Key words Plant Flower Tree Sun Water Feel Smell	Use ready to roll icing, marzipan and food colourings to make 2-D flower shapes (use commercial pastry cutters). Create an edible picture or use them to decorate a cake.	

61

Table 6.4 Example of a subject leader's medium-term planning – Key Stage 1, Access and Extension, Sc2 Growing: green plants

Subject Leader's Medium-term Planning

Key Stage: 1 Access & Extension	Subject: Science	PoS: Sc2 Growing: green plants	Curriculum links: English, Art and design, Geography, Maths	L-TP reference: Year 2 Spring 2
Intended learning outcomes	Activities		Assessment prompts	

Intended learning outcomes	Activities	Assessment prompts
Sc1: Scientific enquiry To develop skills of scientific enquiry through activities which provide opportunities to: • anticipate and make choices • use senses to investigate materials and resources • observe, comment and measure • record and evaluate.	Explore a variety of potted plants. Discuss their properties, e.g. shiny, green, and identify different parts, e.g. leaf, stem, flower. Draw still life images using pastels, chalks or watercolours. *Art and design link* Visit a local park. Take a simple recording sheet, e.g. computer graphics of trees, bushes, flowers, grass. Look for them and circle the images or use a simple tick chart, e.g. 'I spy'. Take photographs for follow-up work. *Geography link*	Pupils may: • handle or observe resources with curiosity and demonstrate a general interest in their properties, features and functions; imitate familiar actions; know that certain actions cause predictable results. *Example:* pressing the trigger on a water spray or exploring seeds and compost in a sand tray. **P4**
Sc2: Life processes and living things *Access* To recognise, identify and name a variety of green plants, e.g. trees and flowers. To recognise, identify and name common parts of green plants.	Read *Jasper's Beanstalk* and make a display. Paint leaves and stems to form an image of the plant. Add to it over the PoS to replicate growth of a real plant. *English link* Visit a garden centre, purchase beans and seeds, e.g. sunflowers, and explore a wide variety of plants. Take digital photographs for follow-up work.	• focus on activities and anticipate actions; explore and group resources with support, and respond to simple scientific questions using their preferred method of communication. *Example:* showing interest in and examining the roots of beans in a jar or commenting on and naming flowers on a visit to a garden centre. **P5**

Intended learning outcomes	Activities	Assessment prompts
To classify flowering and non-flowering plants and trees and observe their differences.	Plant beans in clear plastic bottles (with the neck removed) lined with blotting paper. Discuss the need for water and light. Place some beans in the light, put others in a dark cupboard. Water both regularly, compare and keep a photographic record. *Maths link*	• recognise features of living things and objects; begin to generalise and predict outcomes, and explore resources intentionally and appropriately and group them to simple given criteria. *Example*: predicting that beans will grow when watered regularly or recognising that all flowers have petals. **P6**
Extension To understand the basic requirements of green plants, i.e. water, light and food.	Plant the sunflower seeds; draw up a rota of pupils responsible for caring for them. Measure them as they grow. Make a large sunflower collage (taller than the pupils) and measure the pupils against it. *Art and design link*	• investigate resources purposefully and group them reliably; make observations and offer ideas using simple scientific language; begin to plan, record and evaluate their work with support. *Example*: using the words 'shiny' and 'green' to describe leaves or using digital photographs or picture symbols to make pictorial classifications of trees and flowers. **P7**
To know that plants can grow from seeds.	Paint/print large images of trees. Use to display words, symbols or photographs to make individual 'reading trees'. New words etc. can be added as the pupils learn them.	• make independent contributions to enquiries and answer simple reasoning questions; recognise similarities and differences in the features of living things and properties of objects consistently. *Example*: commenting on which sunflower grew the tallest or recognising that trees are taller than flowers. **P8**
	Cut out individual plant parts, i.e. roots, stem, leaves and flowers. Use sticky-backed Velcro and a felt board or screen. Encourage the pupils to 'construct' an image of a flowering plant. Make labels of the basic parts to add to the picture.	Refer to the National Curriculum guidance for science assessment prompts beyond P8.
Key words Flower Root Plant Stem Tree Leaf Grow Petal Sun/Light Seed Rain/Water Bulb	Make a large collage of a flowering plant above/below ground. Add images of the sun and rain to reinforce the basic needs for plant growth. *Art and design link*	

Table 6.6 Example of a subject leader's medium-term planning – Key Stage 1, Access and Extension, Sc3 Freezing and melting

Subject Leader's Medium-term Planning

Key Stage: 1 Access & Extension	Subject: Science	PoS: Sc3 Freezing and melting	Curriculum links: Maths, DT	L-TP reference: Year 3 Autumn 2
Intended learning outcomes	**Activities**		**Assessment prompts**	

Intended learning outcomes	Activities	Assessment prompts
Sc1: Scientific enquiry To develop skills of scientific enquiry through activities which provide opportunities to: • anticipate and make choices • use senses to investigate materials and resources • observe, comment and measure • record and evaluate. **Sc3: Materials and their properties** **Access** To explore frozen resources actively; observe and comment on their properties (e.g. cold, hard).	Explore a variety of frozen resources, e.g. peas, ice cream, ice cubes. Leave some to thaw and compare to original state. Carry out a fair test with ice cubes. Leave some in a fridge and some in the sun. Record pictorially which melted more in a given time. Use plastic bottles and add a layer of coloured water daily and freeze until the bottle is full of 'rainbow ice'. Investigate how to get the ice out and observe the changes as it melts. Use digital photographs to record the process. *Maths link* Freeze different drinks, e.g. cola, orange juice, milk shake. Carry out a fair test: which drink freezes or melts the fastest? Taste and compare the different states. Fill containers with water to different levels, mark the level with tape or pen and freeze. Check levels once water is frozen: are they higher or lower than before? *Maths link*	Pupils may: • handle or observe resources with curiosity and demonstrate a general interest in their properties, features and functions; imitate familiar actions; know that certain actions cause predictable results. *Example:* observing ice melting when playing in the water tray or pouring chocolate into a mould. **P4** • focus on activities and anticipate actions; explore and group resources with support, and respond to simple scientific questions using their preferred method of communication. *Example:* making a pictogram of familiar frozen foods or being able to answer questions such as 'Is the chocolate hard or soft?' **P5**

Intended learning outcomes	Activities	Assessment prompts
To recognise and name the changes in state of substances when frozen and as they thaw or melt. To predict the outcomes of freezing and melting processes. *Extension* To find out how to reverse changes in state (e.g. ice – water – ice). **Key words** Freezing Melting Hot Cold Ice Water Change Hard Soft Liquid Solid	Examine a variety of familiar foods, e.g. cheese, sliced apple, crisps, chocolate. Encourage the pupils to predict which will melt when heated in a microwave. Compare before and after. Make a pictogram of foods that melt. *DT (Food) link* Find out about materials/resources that help to keep things frozen or warm. Wrap ice or hot toast in e.g. foil, newspaper and cling film, and compare results after 30 minutes. Make chocolate crispy cakes. Melt chocolate in different ways, e.g. in a microwave, leaving in the sun. Observe the changes in state and evaluate the melting methods used. Take digital photographs of the lesson and record the results of the evaluation pictorially or symbolically. *DT (Food) link*	• recognise features of living things and objects; begin to generalise and predict outcomes, and explore resources intentionally and appropriately and group them to simple given criteria. **P6** *Example:* describing the properties of ice or predicting that ice cream will melt in the sun. • investigate resources purposefully and group them reliably; make observations and offer ideas using simple scientific language; begin to plan, record and evaluate their work with support. *Example:* suggesting substances to use in a test about melting or commenting on the level of ice compared with the original level of water in a freezing test. **P7** • make independent contributions to enquiries and answer simple reasoning questions; recognise similarities and differences in the features of living things and properties of objects consistently. **P8** *Example:* suggesting liquids to use in a fair test about freezing or recognising that a microwave is the most effective way of melting chocolate. Refer to the National Curriculum guidance for science assessment prompts beyond P8.

Table 6.7 Example of a class teacher's medium-term planning – Key Stage 1

Class Teacher's Medium-term Planning

Subject: Science			PoS: Sc4 Push and pull toys
Class: Infant 2		Teacher: Chris	Long-term plan ref.: Year 1, Spring 1
Lesson	ILO (F)*	Focus skills (A–E)	Activities *(Three-part lesson)*
1	All pupils encounter and have access to a broad range of sensory experiences and activities presented in a scientific context through which they may demonstrate awareness; respond and show interest; engage and explore indiscriminately; participate intentionally, and initiate involvement.	**Sc1 skill:** Predicting **Key skill:** Turn-taking	Introduction: puppet; cue song; key words/symbols. Make a simple track and race push toys. Predict the winner. Keep simple scores. Plenary: discuss races; recap key words and song.
2		**Sc1 skill:** Observing **Key skill:** Turn-taking	Introduction: puppet; cue song; key words/symbols. Use large push-pull toys. Pupils race them in pairs. Other pupils predict the winner. Keep a score. Plenary: recap key words; discuss results.
3		**Sc1 skill:** Observing **Key skill:** Problem solving	Introduction: puppet; cue song; key words/symbols. Push inflated balloons into buckets of water. Vary sizes and shapes. Plenary: recap key words and song.
4		**Sc1 skill:** Observing **Key skill:** Improving own learning	Introduction: puppet; cue song; key words/symbols. Visit a local park. Observe/experience how different resources move. Take photographs of the visit. Plenary: discuss the experience on return.
5		**Sc1 skill:** Recording **Key skill:** Improving own learning	Introduction: cue song; key words/symbols. Use the photographs of the park visit to record preferences and movements experienced. Plenary: present their work; recap key words.
6		**Sc1 skill:** Measuring **Key skill:** Application of number	Introduction: cue song; key words/symbols. Use large ramp/PE bench. Pupils choose resources to push down. Predict/measure which will go furthest. Plenary: recall which resource won; recap key words.
7		**Sc1 skill:** Problem-solving **Key skill:** Working with others	**Assessment** Play activities: pull-string toys; large/sit-on push-pull toys. Pupils explore activities independently. One-to-one observation of pupils' knowledge/skills.

Science learning outcomes	Cross-curricular links	Key words
To cause movement by pushing and pulling. To name the action used to move a resource. To describe the movements of resources (e.g. 'fast').	Maths	• Push • Go • Pull • Fast • Stop • Move

*ILO(F): Intended learning outcomes (Foundation)

Table 6.8 Example of short-term planning – Key Stage 1

Short-term planning

Subject: Science	**PoS:** Sc4 Push and pull toys	**Date:** 17th Jan.
Cross-curricular links: n/a		**Class:** Infant 2

Intended learning outcomes (*Including key skills*)	**Key words**
Foundation (P1–3) To develop communication and problem-solving skills. To develop cooperative work skills. To be proactive in their sensory exploration of resources. **Access (P4–7)** To experience pushing against a resistant force (i.e. balloons into buckets of water). To use the word/sign 'push' in context. **Extension (P8–NC1/2)** To describe their actions using simple scientific vocabulary.	• Push • Fast • Go

Activities (*Include differentiation for pupils at Foundation, Access and Extension*)

Introduction: cue with 'Sammy Science Snake' puppet. Recap key words; demonstrate investigation.
Split into groups.

Group 1 (Foundation)
Choose colour of balloon; use pump to inflate (with support). Fill buckets with water. Try pushing balloon under water; wait for it to 'pop up'. Build anticipation.

Group 2 (Access)
Select two balloons (large and small) and try to inflate independently. Problem-solve how to fill buckets with water. Try pushing balloons under water; observe what happens to water level. Predict what will happen when they let go of each balloon.

Group 3 (Extension)
As for Access pupils but vary colour, sizes and shape of balloons. Describe what the action feels like with the different balloons.

Plenary: regroup; share experiences and results. Recap key words with 'Sammy'.

Classroom organisation

Group 1	Pervas and Alex	**Staff**	Wendy
Group 2	Lauren, May, Dominic and Aaron	**Staff**	Emma and Vicky
Group 3	Jacob, Keeva and Jamie	**Staff**	Claire

Resources	**IEP targets**
• 'Sammy Snake' • Buckets • Balloons • Pump • 'Push' symbol	**Alex** to sit in ladder-back chair for 10 minutes. **Aaron** to join small group activity for 2 minutes then 'choose'. **Jamie** to name colours (of balloons): red, blue, yellow. **Pervas** to tolerate supported sensory exploration.

Resource list for Key Stage 1

Push and pull toys

Simple recording sheets, for example, Figures 6.2, 6.3 and 6.4.

Large resources for pushing and pulling could include: soft play blocks or cubes; toy boxes (e.g. curver boxes); large sacks filled with toys or sand; home corner resources (e.g. play oven or fridge).

To make a sand bag use a hessian sack or pillowcase and three quarters fill it with sand. Pupils can help to fill this and then problem solve how to move it to a given point and empty it.

Large push and pull toys (e.g. lawn mower, vacuum cleaner) are available from suppliers of primary educational resources and major toyshops such as Early Learning Centre.

Growing

Rose, peppermint and lavender waters are available at herbalist shops and some pharmacies. Ask for advice on dilution measures.

Flower cutters are available from specialist cake shops, department stores and some supermarkets and toy shops.

Dried beans can be purchased at most garden centres.

Jasper's Beanstalk by Nick Butterworth and Mick Inkpen (1992) Hodder Headline, London.

Useful website: www.bbc.co.uk/go/learning/int/banner/-/gardening/children

Figure 6.1 Finding out about growing plants

Tips for growing beans

Use good quality absorbent paper (blotting paper works best). Cover the tops of the cut-down plastic bottles with Clingfilm (with air holes) to speed up propagation.

Rhymes and songs

'Lavenders blue, dilly, dilly'

'Ring o' ring o' roses'

'Mary, Mary, quite contrary'

'In and out the dusky bluebells'

'I had a little nut tree'

Adapted rhyme

1. Here we go round the mulberry bush,
   The mulberry bush, the mulberry bush,
   Here we go round the mulberry bush,
   On a bright and sunny morning.

Other verses

2. This is the way we dig the soil.

3. This is the way we plant the seeds.

4. This is the way we water the plants.

5. Repeat first verse.

Freezing and melting

Simple recording sheets, for example, Figure 6.5.

Chocolate crispy cakes

Ingredients

250g cooking chocolate
75g Rice Crispies

Equipment

Cake cases
Large plastic bowl
Wooden spoons
Teaspoons

Method

Melt the chocolate in a large bowl in the microwave. Do this in short stages to avoid overcooking and to give pupils a turn at programming the microwave.

Once melted stir in the Rice Crispies and then spoon into the cake cases in turn.

Pulling

Toys   I   can   pull.

Pull

Figure 6.2 'Pulling' recording sheet

© Claire Marvin and Chris Stokoe (2003) *Access to Science*, David Fulton Publishers.

Pushing

Toys   I   can   push.

Push

Figure 6.3 'Pushing' recording sheet

© Claire Marvin and Chris Stokoe (2003) *Access to Science*, David Fulton Publishers.

Pushing   and   pulling

At   the   park   I   liked:

Name: _____

Figure 6.4 'Pushing and pulling' recording sheet

© Claire Marvin and Chris Stokoe (2003) *Access to Science*, David Fulton Publishers.

Melting

Food   that   melts   in   a   microwave.

Name: _____

Figure 6.5 'Melting' recording sheet

CHAPTER SEVEN

Practical materials for Key Stage 2

Experiences and opportunities at Key Stage 2

The focus of teaching science at Key Stage 2 may be on giving pupils opportunities to:

- begin to plan, carry out and evaluate simple investigations in familiar surroundings using key skills for learning, for example, sensory awareness, problem solving
- explore and investigate their local environment in order to gain greater awareness, knowledge and understanding of the wider world including themselves.

Given these opportunities in science at Key Stage 2 the QCA/DfEE (2001a: 15) guidelines suggest that:

all pupils with learning difficulties (including those with the most profound disabilities)	continue to develop their experience and understanding of the world by using their senses, observing and exploring. With appropriate support, they take part in investigations about living things, materials and phenomena. They gain greater awareness of life processes and of themselves as growing and changing individuals.
most pupils with learning difficulties (including those with severe difficulties in learning) who will develop further skills, knowledge and understanding in most aspects of the subject	learn about a wider range of living things, materials and phenomena. They carry out investigations with others and collect evidence, become familiar with some reference sources, record their results, *for example, using objects, symbols or computer software*, and communicate what they have done and what happened. They use some scientific language and answer scientific questions.
a few pupils with learning difficulties who will develop further aspects of knowledge, skills and understanding in the subject	attempt to answer questions through testing and investigating. They ask scientific questions, use some reference sources, drawings, charts and diagrams to communicate their findings and ideas. They recognise relevant evidence and evaluate it, draw conclusions from their data, consider if tests are fair or unfair, and link their scientific knowledge to their everyday experiences.

Learning opportunities at Key Stage 2

Tables 7.1–7.8 are examples of a subject leader's medium-term plans for science-focused units of work at Key Stage 2 covered over a term or half a term. These are followed by Table 7.9, an example of a class teacher's planning sheet for a series of weekly lessons from a selected unit of work, and Table 7.10, a short-term plan exemplifying a single session from within the series.

Table 7.1 Example of a subject leader's medium-term planning – Key Stage 2, Foundation, Sc2 Mini-beasts

Subject Leader's Medium-term Planning

Key Stage: 2 Foundation	Subject: Science	PoS: Sc2 Mini-beasts	Curriculum links: ICT, Art and design	L-TP reference: Year 1 Summer 2
Intended learning outcomes	Activities		Assessment prompts	
Sc1: Scientific enquiry All pupils will encounter a range of scientific experiences and sensory resources linked to the programme of study. These opportunities will provide a context in which pupils learn to:	Introduce the PoS by using a selection of fabrics and materials to represent characteristics of mini-beasts, e.g. silk or organza for wings, fur fabric and gloves for spider's body and legs. Recite rhymes or poems or sing songs about mini-beasts, e.g. 'Incy wincy spider', 'Ladybird, ladybird', and use the fabrics or materials to illustrate the rhymes and actions, e.g. 'walking' gloved fingers gently on pupil's hand.		Pupils may:	
			• demonstrate simple reflex responses and be resistant or passive to supported sensory activities. *Example:* taking part in a visit to a butterfly farm or making resistant movements when stroked with fur fabric. **P1(i)**	
• demonstrate emerging awareness **P1(ii)**	Present a selection of interactive mini-beast toys, e.g. large spider on elastic or clockwork ladybird. Let the pupils explore them and indicate their preference. Hide their choices under fabrics or in a box filled with leaves or grass and encourage the pupils to search for them.		• focus their attention briefly on people, objects and events, and give intermittent reactions. *Example:* focusing their attention briefly during an activity to select materials for a mini-beast display or recoiling from the feel of cold spaghetti used to represent worms. **P1(ii)**	
• respond and show interest **P2(i)**				
• engage and explore indiscriminately **P2(ii)**	Experience lying on the grass in the sun and in the shade. Cover the pupils with blankets or soft fabrics to simulate mini-beasts' habitat.		• accept and engage in supported exploration and reject or begin to show interest in new and unfamiliar activities and resources. *Example:* leaning forwards to look at a spider in a glass tank or coactively exploring the textures of fabrics used to reinforce mini-beast rhymes. **P2(i)**	
• participate intentionally **P3(i)**	Plan a visit to a butterfly farm or wildlife centre. Record the visit using video or digital camera. Use for follow-up work.			
• initiate involvement. **P3(ii)**	Make butterfly cakes or use mini-rolls decorated to look like caterpillars. Use a food mixer to make the cakes, let the pupils operate the appliance using large switch. *ICT link*			

Intended learning outcomes	Activities	Assessment prompts
	Make symmetrical splash paintings to form butterfly images. *Art and design link*	• interact with people and begin to explore objects proactively; perform actions through supported trial and error and communicate preferences and dislikes. *Example:* exploring the textures of grass and leaves during an activity simulating mini-beast habitats or working cooperatively to produce a splash painting of a butterfly. **P2(ii)**
	Experience feeling soil, sand, mud, grass, leaves and branches. Use these materials to make a collage picture of mini-beast habitats. Make 2-D collages and 3-D models of mini-beasts to form a display. *Art and design link*	
	Watch extracts of TV programmes or films about mini-beasts, e.g. *A Bug's Life* or *Spider in the Bath* and record pupils' favourite parts. *ICT link*	• begin to show interest in and observe the results of their actions; choose to interact with people actively, and explore objects with less support. *Example:* joining in and imitating actions with support during rhymes about mini-beasts or showing interest in the movements of butterflies during a visit to a butterfly farm. **P3(i)**
	Explore a selection of resources such as cold spaghetti (for 'worms'), snail shells filled with Playdough or 'slime' (for 'snails'), wet marshmallows (for 'slugs'). Record the pupils' responses.	
	Present a selection of battery-operated, pneumatic or audio-response mini-beast toys. Encourage the pupils to investigate how to operate them and cause the movement, sound or vibration. *ICT link*	• explore objects independently for short periods and initiate interactions with people; demonstrate an emerging potential to solve simple problems and begin to anticipate the outcomes of activities. *Example:* anticipating the action of a favourite mini-beast toy or filling and emptying a container with materials used to simulate mini-beast habitats to search for a favourite resource. **P3(ii)**
Key words Worm Spider Feel Snail Slug Butterfly	Invite a mini-beast specialist into school. Pupils experience observing or handling the mini-beasts. Make a photographic book to record the pupils' responses and to share with peers as a library resource.	

Table 7.2 Example of a subject leader's medium-term planning – Key Stage 2, Access and Extension, Sc2 Mini-beasts

Subject Leader's Medium-term Planning

Key Stage: 2 Access & Extension	Subject: Science	PoS: Sc2 Mini-beasts	Curriculum links: Maths, Art and design, English, ICT	L-TP reference: Year 1 Summer 2
Intended learning outcomes	Activities		Assessment prompts	

Intended learning outcomes	Activities	Assessment prompts
Sc1: Scientific enquiry To develop skills of scientific enquiry through activities which provide opportunities to: • anticipate and make choices • use senses to investigate materials and resources • observe, comment and measure • record and evaluate. **Sc2: Life processes and living things** *Access* To recognise differences between types of mini-beast. To group classes of mini-beast to simple criteria. To find out about the natural environments and habitats of mini-beasts.	Examine a selection of pictures, photographs and books about mini-beasts. Use 3-D models (toys) of mini-beasts and hide them in layers of compost, leaves or tissue paper. Encourage the pupils to search for them and as they find them, place them in sets, e.g. 'spiders', 'ladybirds'. *Maths link* Use a square of plastic and peg it out on a grassed area and leave it for two weeks. Explain to the pupils that they are making a 'house for mini-beasts'. Go back and check, take photographs of any 'inhabitants'. Use magnifying glasses to study them closely. Use secondary sources to find out about the mini-beasts found. 'Grow' sea monkeys. Find out how to care for them, what they are. Write a fact sheet about them and make a rota to care for them. Encourage the pupils to choose one type of mini-beast to find out about. Use secondary sources to research the mini-beast, e.g. habitat, eating habits, life cycle.	Pupils may: • handle or observe resources with curiosity and demonstrate a general interest in their properties, features and functions; imitate familiar actions; know that certain actions cause predictable results. *Example*: searching for models of mini-beasts in a sand tray filled with leaves and compost or joining in with action rhymes about mini-beasts. **P4** • focus on activities and anticipate actions; explore and group resources with support, and respond to simple scientific questions using their preferred method of communication. *Example*: making simple sets of mini-beast models or pictorial representations or helping to dig for worms for the wormery. **P5** • recognise features of living things and objects; begin to generalise and predict outcomes, and explore resources intentionally and appropriately and group them to simple given criteria. *Example*: grouping winged and non-winged mini-beasts or observing and commenting on the worms' behaviour in the wormery. **P6**

Intended learning outcomes	Activities	Assessment prompts
Extension To take responsibility for caring for the mini-beasts collected.	Make a 'wormery' using layers of soil and sand in a perspex container (or commercial wormery). Find out how to make a wormery, e.g. visit a library and use books and CD-ROMs, or use the Internet. *ICT link*	• investigate resources purposefully and group them reliably; make observations and offer ideas using simple scientific language; begin to plan, record and evaluate their work with support. *Example:* examining the mini-beasts found under the plastic cover and identifying them with support or finding out how to regenerate sea monkeys and knowing they need to be fed. **P7**
To investigate how the natural environment supplies the needs of mini-beasts.	Use picture symbols to produce a 'Snap' or 'Lotto' game of different mini-beasts and play together in small groups.	
	Make 2- or 3-D collage images of mini-beasts to form a display. Hang some on elastic, e.g. butterflies, bees. *Art and design link*	• make independent contributions to enquiries and answer simple reasoning questions; recognise similarities and differences in the features of living things and properties of objects consistently. *Example:* classifying spiders, insects and invertebrates to given criteria or observing and commenting on the behaviour of pond life during a visit to a wildlife centre. **P8**
	Go on a visit to a natural wildlife centre. Experience pond dipping. Collect pond life, and use magnifying glasses to study it closely. Take video or digital photographs for follow-up work.	
	Make a tactile book of favourite mini-beasts for the library.	
	Read stories about mini-beasts, e.g. *The Very Busy Spider* and *The Very Hungry Caterpillar*. Use soft and interactive toys to illustrate the stories. Alternatively sing songs or say rhymes, e.g. 'Incy wincy spider', to reinforce the names of specific mini-beasts. *English link*	
Key words Insect Worm Mini-beast Soil Spider Home Water Wings Caterpillar Legs	Make pictorial sets or worksheets of insects, spiders and invertebrates. Write about the simple distinguishing features, e.g. 'how many legs?', 'wings or no wings?', and their natural habitats, e.g. wet or dry places.	Refer to the National Curriculum guidance for science assessment prompts beyond P8.

Table 7.3 Example of a subject leader's medium-term planning – Key Stage 2, Foundation, Sc2 Skeletons

Subject Leader's Medium-term Planning

Key Stage: 2 Foundation	Subject: Science	PoS: Sc2 Skeletons	Curriculum links: Music	L-TP reference: Year 2 Autumn 2
Intended learning outcomes	**Activities**		**Assessment prompts**	
Sc1: Scientific enquiry All pupils will encounter a range of scientific experiences and sensory resources linked to the programme of study. These opportunities will provide a context in which pupils learn to:	Introduce the PoS by using gentle massage to assist identification of body parts, i.e. hands and feet. Concentrate on knuckles, ankles and wrists.		Pupils may:	
• demonstrate emerging awareness **P1(ii)**	Make skeleton/'Funny Bones' mobile using tactile materials. Encourage pupils to explore and select preferred textures. Use materials to wrap around hands and feet.		• demonstrate simple reflex responses and be resistant or passive to supported sensory activities. *Example:* remaining passive during hand massage or startling to the sound of claves on a resonance board. **P1(i)**	
• respond and show interest **P2(i)**	Use blankets, parachute, trampet (small trampoline), PE ball to enable pupils to experience gross-motor movements in both jerky and smooth styles. Use pre-recorded music to accompany movements, e.g. 'Fossils' (jerky) and 'The Swan' (smooth) from Camille Saint-Saëns' *Carnival of the Animals.* *Music link*		• focus their attention briefly on people, objects and events, and give intermittent reactions. *Example:* looking briefly at a projected image in the multisensory area or demonstrating a change in body tone when moved in a blanket. **P1(ii)**	
• engage and explore indiscriminately **P2(ii)**				
• participate intentionally **P3(i)**	Place pupils on a resonance board. Use claves and beaters to make skeleton noises – let pupils experience, sounds and vibrations.		• accept and engage in supported exploration and reject or begin to show interest in new and unfamiliar activities and resources. *Example:* making a fluorescent handprint with support or rejecting a foot massage. **P2(i)**	
• initiate involvement. **P3(ii)**	Use a projector or OHP to create skeleton images in the multisensory area. Play music with staccato quality (e.g. glockenspiel, wood-blocks). *Music link*			

Intended learning outcomes	Activities	Assessment prompts
	Make hand and footprints in monochrome to create an 'X-ray' effect.	• interact with people and begin to explore objects proactively; perform actions through supported trial and error and communicate preferences and dislikes.
	Splash fluorescent paint onto black fabric or paper body outlines. Or do it on old T-shirts and gloves, let pupils wear them in multisensory area and look at own image in a mirror.	*Example*: splashing fluorescent paint onto a T-shirt or gloves with support or leaning forward to watch the movement of projected skeleton images. **P2(ii)**
	Hide resources in boxes or 'feely-bags'. Encourage the pupils to search for what is inside. Use hard objects such as candlesticks or rolling pins to simulate bones.	• begin to show interest in and observe the results of their actions; choose to interact with people actively, and explore objects with less support.
		Example: communicating enjoyment while being moved in a jerky way in a parachute or exploring the contents of a 'feely-bag'. **P3(i)**
		• explore objects independently for short periods and initiate interactions with people; demonstrate an emerging potential to solve simple problems and begin to anticipate the outcomes of activities.
		Example: exploring and choosing tactile materials to make a skeleton image or anticipating their movement when placed on a PE ball. **P3(ii)**
Key words Feel Body Head Hands Feet		

Table 7.4 Example of a subject leader's medium-term planning – Key Stage 2, Access and Extension, Sc2 Skeletons

Subject Leader's Medium-term Planning

Key Stage: 2 Access & Extension	Subject: Science	PoS: Sc2 Skeletons	Curriculum links: English, ICT, PSHE, DT	L-TP reference: Year 2 Autumn 2
Intended learning outcomes	**Activities**		**Assessment prompts**	
Sc1: Scientific enquiry To develop skills of scientific enquiry through activities which provide opportunities to: • anticipate and make choices • use senses to investigate materials and resources • observe, comment and measure • record and evaluate.	Use a model of a skeleton (Figure 7.5), look at pictures and images, feel own bones, e.g. wrist, kneecap. Talk about properties and purpose of skeleton, e.g. to keep us upright, help us move, protect internal organs. Paint or draw monochrome images of skeletons using the resources to prompt ideas. Make a game 'Skeletons' (as 'Beetle'). Use black card to make laminated body outlines, cut out long and short bones, skull, rib cage – number them and position on body outline; use a large die to play the game. (Use Velcro to place the 'bones'.)		Pupils may: • handle or observe resources with curiosity and demonstrate a general interest in their properties, features and functions; imitate familiar actions; know that certain actions cause predictable results. *Example:* pointing to familiar body parts (e.g. head) with support or indicating a preference for a preferred calcium-rich food. **P4**	
Sc2: Life processes and living things **Access** To locate familiar body parts.	Watch extract of *Funny Bones* video or listen to tape. Make up own 'Funny Bones' story, act it out, use skeleton masks or make own using 'Modroc'. *English link*		• focus on activities and anticipate actions; explore and group resources with support, and respond to simple scientific questions using their preferred method of communication. *Example:* pointing to body parts on request or saying which body parts feel hard and which soft. **P5**	
To know that they have bones inside their bodies. To name simple parts of skeletons, e.g. bones, skull.	Investigate different ways of moving and positioning their bodies, e.g. curling, stretching, waving. Draw round the pupils in their chosen position. Use black paper and white chalk. Cut out the body image and involve pupils in adding outlines of bones (e.g. long bones, skull, rib cage) to produce a skeleton image for display.		• recognise features of living things and objects; begin to generalise and predict outcomes, and explore resources intentionally and appropriately and group them to simple given criteria. *Example:* knowing that humans have unseen skeletons or knowing that bones are hard. **P6**	

P7

nt prompts

ate resources purposefully and group them
make observations and offer ideas using
scientific language; begin to plan, record and
their work with support.
eing able to use the words 'skeleton' or
n context or recognising and grouping foods
good for maintaining healthy bones.

P8

ependent contributions to enquiries and
mple reasoning questions; recognise
s and differences in the features of living
properties of objects consistently.
mparing the sizes of skeletons observed
isit to a natural history museum or
g on the properties of a human skeleton
g a CD-ROM package.

...eating to help keep bones strong.

Go on a visit to a natural history museum to look at
skeletons of humans and animals. Make a simple
recording sheet of things you expect the pupils to
observe. Take photographs of the visit, use recording
and photographic evidence for follow-up work, e.g.
make a book about the visit.

Use simple software packages to view the skeletal
system and to reinforce the concept of the skeleton as
an internal structure and its functions (see KS2
resource list).

ICT link

Refer to the National Curriculum guidance for science
assessment prompts beyond P8.

Key words

Skeleton	Bone
Hard	Soft
Body	Skull
Ribs	Spine
Inside	

Table 7.5 Example of a subject leader's medium-term planning – Key Stage 2, Foundation, Sc4 Electricity

Subject Leader's Medium-term Planning

Key Stage: 2 Foundation	Subject: Science	PoS: Sc4 Electricity	Curriculum links: ICT, Music	L-TP reference: Year 3 Spring 1
Intended learning outcomes	Activities		Assessment prompts	
Sc1: Scientific enquiry All pupils will encounter a range of scientific experiences and sensory resources linked to the programme of study. These opportunities will provide a context in which pupils learn to: • demonstrate emerging awareness **P1(ii)** • respond and show interest **P2(i)** • engage and explore indiscriminately **P2(ii)** • participate intentionally **P3(i)** • initiate involvement. **P3(ii)**	Introduce the programme of study by using vibrating and auditory battery-operated resources. Hide them under blankets or in boxes and encourage the pupils to use their senses to search for them. Present a range of electrical cause and effect resources, e.g. remote control cars, massage cushion, and arrange as an activity circuit. Let the pupils experience each in turn. Encourage the pupils to make choices and operate. Take digital photographs or video their involvement. Keep a record of pupils' preferences for use as leisure activities. Use a Soundbeam to enable the pupils to compose electronic music through reflex or intentional body movements. *Music link* Use an electric blender operated by a large switch to make milk shakes using milk, ice cream and different soft fruits, e.g. bananas, strawberries. Taste the different drinks and encourage the pupils to choose their favourite. *ICT link*		Within a scientific context pupils may: • demonstrate simple reflex responses and be resistant or passive to supported sensory activities. *Example:* startling to the sound of corn popping in the microwave or resisting having their feet placed in a foot spa. **P1(i)** • focus their attention briefly on people, objects and events, and give intermittent reactions. *Example:* giving fleeting attention to the lights changing in the infinity tunnel or turning in response to the sound of an electric mixer. **P1(ii)** • accept and engage in supported exploration and reject or begin to show interest in new and unfamiliar activities and resources. *Example:* tolerating tasting different milk shakes or discarding a battery-operated toy in favour of a preferred resource. **P2(i)**	

Intended learning outcomes	Activities	Assessment prompts
	Use large switches to operate multisensory equipment, e.g. foot spa, infinity tunnel, fan. Pupils experience each activity in turn. Record preferences and dislikes for personal profiles. *ICT link*	• interact with people and begin to explore objects proactively; perform actions through supported trial and error and communicate preferences and dislikes. *Example:* rocking in response to a favourite piece of music or operating a light source in the multisensory area with support or by trial and error.　**P2(ii)**
	Make popcorn in a microwave oven operated by a large switch. Listen to the popping noise as it cooks and wait for it to stop. Use their senses to explore the finished produce. *ICT link*	• begin to show interest in and observe the results of their actions; choose to interact with people actively, and explore objects with less support. *Example:* indicating a preference for a particular resource in the multisensory area consistently or focusing attention on a moving electrical toy for a short period.　**P3(i)**
	Listen to a selection of music recordings on CDs. Encourage the pupils to communicate their preferences and use a large switch to listen to their favourite tracks again. Keep a record of pupil preferences to use during leisure activities. *Music link*	• explore objects independently for short periods and initiate interactions with people; demonstrate an emerging potential to solve simple problems and begin to anticipate the outcomes of activities. *Example:* searching purposefully for an auditory resource hidden under a blanket or anticipating the opportunity to play with a favourite electrical resource by, for example, vocalising or clapping as it is presented.　**P3(ii)**
Key words Listen　Feel Look　Taste Smell　Switch On　Off		

Table 7.6 Example of a subject leader's medium-term planning – Key Stage 2, Access and Extension, Sc4 Electricity

Subject Leader's Medium-term Planning

Key Stage: 2 Access & Extension	Subject: Science	PoS: Sc4 Electricity	Curriculum links: Maths, PSHE	L-TP reference: Year 3 Spring 1
Intended learning outcomes	**Activities**		**Assessment prompts**	
Sc1: Scientific enquiry To develop skills of scientific enquiry through activities which provide opportunities to: • anticipate and make choices • use senses to investigate materials and resources • observe, comment and measure • record and evaluate.	Demonstrate use of electrical appliances or toys, e.g. foot spa, 'Scalextric'. Show the pupils that you have to make them work by plugging them into electrical sockets. Reinforce the safety rules as you do so. Switch the resource on and off to demonstrate that the electrical supply is making it work. Encourage the pupils to investigate how the resources work. *PSHE link* Go on an investigative tour of the classroom or school environment. Find out how many electrical appliances there are. Make a pictogram of the results using picture symbols or catalogue images. *Maths link*		Pupils may: • handle or observe resources with curiosity and demonstrate a general interest in their properties, features and functions; imitate familiar actions; know that certain actions cause predictable results. *Example:* pressing a switch to operate an electric whisk or watching the movement of remote control toys. **P4** • focus on activities and anticipate actions; explore and group resources with support, and respond to simple scientific questions using their preferred method of communication. *Example:* knowing that the fridge is cold inside or grouping a selection of familiar light sources. **P5**	
Sc4: Physical processes **Access** To know the basic safety rules when using electrical equipment. To know that they can cause an action by operating the switch on an appliance. To recognise that familiar appliances need electrical power to function.	Go on a visit to a large electrical retail supplier. Make 'I spy' worksheets depicting familiar electrical appliances so the pupils can record what they see. Make models of common electrical appliances, e.g. fridge or cooker. Discuss how electricity makes these appliances work and find out what their function is.		• recognise features of living things and objects; begin to generalise and predict outcomes, and explore resources intentionally and appropriately and group them to simple given criteria. *Example:* identifying which resources need batteries to make them work or predicting that the electric whisk will work faster than the hand whisk. **P6**	

Intended learning outcomes	Activities	Assessment prompts
Extension To operate and use a range of electrical resources with minimal support safely.	Make instant desserts using whisks. Carry out a fair test to compare the effectiveness of using a hand whisk and an electric whisk. Predict which will make the dessert the fastest. Use digital photographs of the process to support follow-up work. Present a selection of interactive battery-operated and mechanical toys. Encourage the pupils to group them and find out how they work. Investigate a selection of battery-operated resources. Present them to the pupils without the batteries fitted. Ask them to find out how to turn them on and if they work. Encourage the pupils to suggest what they need to make them work. Demonstrate how to fit the batteries and let the pupils fit them with support, and test them to see if they work. Visit an 'eco centre' or wind farm to observe the natural production of electricity. Use digital photographs to record the visit for follow-up work. Conduct an investigation to find out about natural sources of electrical power in order to operate a clock.	• investigate resources purposefully and group them reliably; make observations and offer ideas using simple scientific language; begin to plan, record and evaluate their work with support. *Example:* grouping common household electrical appliances or completing an 'I spy' worksheet of familiar appliances with minimal support. **P7** • make independent contributions to enquiries and answer simple reasoning questions; recognise similarities and differences in the features of living things and properties of objects consistently. *Example:* comparing the effectiveness of the electrical whisk with the hand whisk or choosing an appropriate appliance for a specific task or function (e.g. cassette player to listen to an audio tape). **P8** Refer to the National Curriculum guidance for science assessment prompts beyond P8.
Key words Electricity Battery Power Work Switch On Off Safe Plug Dangerous		

89

Table 7.7 Example of a subject leader's medium-term planning – Key Stage 2, Foundation, Sc3 Washing and drying

Subject Leader's Medium-term Planning

Key Stage: 2 Foundation	Subject: Science	PoS: Sc3 Washing and drying	Curriculum links: PSHE, Maths, Art and design, ICT	L-TP reference: Year 4 Summer 2
Intended learning outcomes	**Activities**		**Assessment prompts**	
Sc1: Scientific enquiry All pupils will encounter a range of scientific experiences and sensory resources linked to the programme of study. These opportunities will provide a context in which pupils learn to: • demonstrate emerging awareness **P1(ii)** • respond and show interest **P2(i)** • engage and explore indiscriminately **P2(ii)** • participate intentionally **P3(i)** • initiate involvement. **P3(ii)**	Introduce the PoS by investigating a selection of fabrics, e.g. silk, velvet, wool, cotton. Encourage the pupils to explore the textures. Spray the fabrics with warm water and let the pupils feel and smell them wet. Alternate wet fabrics with dry and record preferences and dislikes. Feel and smell different washing powders and liquids (check for toxicity). Record pupils' preferences. Mix washing powders with colourings and bicarbonate of soda to make it foam. Role-play a tea party; make a mess on the table cloth and napkins, then hand wash using pupils' preferred washing substance. Use baby-sized dolls and role-play bathing and drying the baby. Use baby lotions and powders and soft warm towels. Encourage and help the pupils to wash and dry their hands and faces using warm and naturally scented fabrics. Reinforce names of body parts as you help them; use a mirror. *PSHE link*		Pupils may: • demonstrate simple reflex responses and be resistant or passive to supported sensory activities. *Example:* startling to the feel of warm water sprayed onto the backs of their hands or eye flickering in response to feel of cold air from hair dryer. **P1(i)** • focus their attention briefly on people, objects and events, and give intermittent reactions. *Example:* giving fleeting attention to a doll's face or recoiling from the feel of wet fabrics. **P1(ii)** • accept and engage in supported exploration and reject or begin to show interest in new and unfamiliar activities and resources. *Example:* accepting the supported exploration of wet and dry fabric or showing interest in the movement of fabrics being dried by a fan. **P2(i)**	

Intended learning outcomes	Activities	Assessment prompts
	Hang wet cloths, e.g. tablecloths, on a washing line. Walk or wheel the pupils in and out of the wet washing. Sing 'In and out the dripping washing'.	• interact with people and begin to explore objects proactively; perform actions through supported trial and error and communicate preferences and dislikes. *Example*: demonstrating dislike of the smells of washing powders or liquids or pressing a large switch to activate a hair dryer with support. **P2(ii)**
	Make a collage of washing hanging on a line using alternating colours – with wind and sun images to help reinforce how fabrics dry outdoors. *Maths & Art and design links*	• begin to show interest in and observe the results of their actions; choose to interact with people actively, and explore objects with less support.
	Experience loading and emptying a washing machine and tumble dryer. Let the pupils feel the vibrations of the machines working.	*Example*: interacting with the resources when role-playing bathing a baby or communicating pleasure when moving in and out of wet washing on a line. **P3(i)**
	Use a 'feely-box' to explore wet and dry resources. Use sponges, chamois leather, fur. Record the pupils' responses, e.g. preferences, anticipation.	• explore objects independently for short periods and initiate interactions with people; demonstrate an emerging potential to solve simple problems and begin to anticipate the outcomes of activities.
	Use a hair dryer, or fan, with a large switch pad to dry samples of wet fabrics or materials. Explore and observe their changing states. *ICT link*	*Example*: attempting to open the door of a washing machine or actively exploring the resources used to wash their faces and hands. **P3(ii)**
Key words Feel Smell Wet Dry Wash Water		

91

Table 7.8 Example of a subject leader's medium-term planning – Key Stage 2, Access and Extension, Sc3 Washing and drying

Subject Leader's Medium-term Planning

Key Stage: 2 Access & Extension	Subject: Science	PoS: Sc3 Washing and drying	Curriculum links: History, Maths, Art and design, English	L-TP reference: Year 4 Summer 2
Intended learning outcomes	**Activities**		**Assessment prompts**	
Sc1: Scientific enquiry To develop skills of scientific enquiry through activities which provide opportunities to: • anticipate and make choices • use senses to investigate materials and resources • observe, comment and measure • record and evaluate.	Experiment with different materials, e.g. tissue, cellophane, blotting paper. Use a water spray and coloured water to wet the materials. Peg the materials on a line and use a hair dryer to dry them, compare with originals and evaluate the outcomes. Use scraps of plain neutral fabrics; stain them with a variety of natural substances, e.g. beetroot, turmeric, tea. Use different methods to wash out the stain, e.g. salt and cold water, or soap flakes. Carry out a fair test on the fabrics and stains to find out which method worked the best.		Pupils may: • handle or observe resources with curiosity and demonstrate a general interest in their properties, features and functions; imitate familiar actions; know that certain actions cause predictable results. *Example:* squeezing water out of fabric before hanging it on a washing line or pressing a switch on a washing machine or tumble dryer to make it work. **P4** • focus on activities and anticipate actions; explore and group resources with support, and respond to simple scientific questions using their preferred method of communication. *Example:* pointing to a clean or dirty cloth on request or sorting wet and dry fabric. **P5**	
Sc3: Materials and their properties *Access* To distinguish between wet and dry materials. To recognise when clothes are dirty and when they are clean. To know that clothes are washed and dried to make them clean.	Make stains on old clothes; wash some by hand and some by machine. Make comparisons and record the results. Research different methods of washing clothes. Compare modern and historical methods, e.g. washboard and soap block. Evaluate the effectiveness of each method and decide whether the test was fair or unfair. *History link*		• recognise features of living things and objects; begin to generalise and predict outcomes, and explore resources intentionally and appropriately and group them to simple given criteria. *Example:* predicting that the washing machine will clean the clothes best or observing and commenting on changes in fabric colour when dyed. **P6**	

Intended learning outcomes	Activities	Assessment prompts
Extension To identify different washing and drying methods.	Hand wash fabric samples and dry using different methods, e.g. make a clothes line outside, use a tumble dryer, dry on a clothes horse in the classroom. Let pupils investigate the drying process and record how long each item took to dry. *Maths link* Use cold-water dyes. Tie-dye different fabrics to make colour changes and patterns. Dry the samples and compare to the originals, how have they changed? Decide which the pupils like the best and why. Use sketchbooks to copy the patterns made by the dyes. Use a digital camera to record the process. *Art and design link* Plan and carry out a visit to a launderette. Take photographs of people doing their laundry. Discuss the sensory experience. Record pupils' responses for follow-up work, e.g. compose a poem or a simple song, draw pictures. *English link*	• investigate resources purposefully and group them reliably; make observations and offer ideas using simple scientific language; begin to plan, record and evaluate their work with support. *Example:* making pictorial records of the results of a fair test to find the best washing method or planning the resources they will need to hand wash clothes. **P7** • make independent contributions to enquiries and answer simple reasoning questions; recognise similarities and differences in the features of living things and properties of objects consistently. *Example:* using secondary sources to find out about historical methods of washing clothes or describing the changes to a fabric when dyed. **P8** Refer to the National Curriculum guidance for science assessment prompts beyond P8.
Key words Wet Dry Dirty Clean Wash Soap Water		

93

Table 7.9 Example of a class teacher's medium-term planning – Key Stage 2

Class Teacher's Medium-term Planning

Subject: Science			PoS: Sc4 Washing and drying
Class: Junior 2		Teacher: Claire	Long-term plan ref.: Year 4, Summer 2
Lesson	ILO (F)*	Focus skills (A–E)	Activities *(Three-part lesson)*
1	All pupils encounter and have access to a broad range of sensory experiences and activities presented in a scientific context through which they may demonstrate awareness; respond and show interest; engage and explore indiscriminately; participate intentionally, and initiate involvement.	**Sc1 skill:** Observing **Key skill:** Turn-taking	Introduction: cue song; key words/symbols. Explore wet/dry fabrics in feely-box. Plenary: sort wet/dry into labelled buckets.
2		**Sc1 skill:** Comparing **Key skill:** Problem solving	Introduction: cue song; key words/symbols. Explore and group wet/dry clothes; hang on a line to dry inside and out. Compare outcomes. Plenary: recap key words; discuss results.
3		**Sc1 skill:** Comparing **Key skill:** Problem solving	Introduction: cue song; key words/symbols. Messy tea party. Wash tablecloths and napkins by hand and machine. Plenary: compare results; recap key words.
4		**Sc1 skill:** Recording **Key skill:** Improving own learning	Introduction: cue song; key words/symbols. Visit a launderette. Complete a recording sheet of observations. Plenary: discuss the experience on return.
5		**Sc1 skill:** Recording **Key skill:** Working with others	Introduction: cue song; key words/symbols. Use photographs/symbols of the visit and washing resources to stimulate ideas for a poem. Plenary: share the poem.
6		**Sc1 skill:** Testing **Key skill:** Problem solving	Introduction: cue song; key words/symbols. Fair test: make stains on like fabrics; use different methods to wash them. Plenary: compare results; record best method.
7		**Sc1 skill:** Problem solving **Key skill:** Working with others	**Assessment** Play activities: washing clothes; bathing a 'baby'; making stains and washing; hanging on a line. One-to-one observation of pupils' knowledge/skills.

Science learning outcomes	Cross-curricular links	Key words
To distinguish between wet/dry; clean/dirty. To know why clothes are washed. To identify different washing and drying methods.	English	• Wash • Dry • Clean • Dirty • Wet • Water

*ILO(F): Intended learning outcomes (Foundation)

Table 7.10 Example of short-term planning – Key Stage 2

Short-term planning

Subject: Science	**PoS:** Sc3 Washing and drying	**Date:** 17th May
Cross-curricular links: n/a		**Class:** Junior 2

Intended learning outcomes (*Including key skills*)	**Key words**
Foundation (P1–3) To develop communication and problem-solving skills. To develop cooperative work skills. To be proactive in their sensory exploration of resources. **Access (P4–7)** To develop problem-solving skills. To differentiate between wet/dry and clean/dirty. **Extension (P8–NC1/2)** To learn about fair tests. To recognise and record which cleaning method worked best.	• Wet • Dry • Clean • Dirty

Activities (*Include differentiation for pupils at Foundation, Access and Extension*)

Introduction: sing cue song, read key words/ symbols.
Explore materials and resources and listen to instructions.
Split into groups.

Group 1 (Foundation)
Pupils use water tray: make stains on fabric squares and then wash in tray; add soap flakes to create bubbles and scent to water. Check to see if stains have gone, i.e. clean or dirty.

Group 2 (Access)
Pupils select fabric squares and decide what to make stains with. Mark fabric and wash first in cold water, then warm. Repeat using soap flakes. Observe changes in state; say whether clothes are clean or dirty.

Group 3 (Extension)
Select fabrics, stain and wash. Use two methods; record which worked best.
Plenary: examine results of tests and group fabric samples into clean and dirty sets. Agree on best method.

Classroom organisation

Group 1	Stephen, Ryan and Harry	**Staff**	Nicola and Julie
Group 2	Paul, Daniel, Rebecca and Jenny	**Staff**	Lorraine and Dave
Group 3	James, Robert and Katie	**Staff**	Chris

Resources	**IEP targets**	
• Calico squares • Water tray/bowls • Soap flakes • Jam • Coffee • Blackcurrant juice	**Stephen** **Ryan** **Harry** **Katie**	to cooperate on staff-directed tasks for 3 minutes. to join in with a whole-group activity for 3 minutes to respond to the 'work together' instruction on his timetable. to name her worksheet independently.

Resource list for Key Stage 2

Mini-beasts

The Very Hungry Caterpillar by Eric Carle (2002) Longman (Pearson Education), Harlow.

The Very Busy Spider by Eric Carle (1996) Hamish Hamilton, Penguin Books, Middlesex.

The Bad Tempered Ladybird by Eric Carle (1977) Penguin, London.

Spider in the Bath (BBC video)

A Bug's Life (Disney video)

Sea monkey kits are available in toy shops and some supermarkets (within the toy department). For further information visit: www.sea-monkeys.com

An investigation of the habitats of mini-beasts and other animals may include the use of simple equipment, for example, beating tray and stick (use stick to give tree branches a few sharp taps; mini-beasts will fall into tray held below), magnifying boxes (place mini-beasts in box and observe through magnified lid) and binoculars (see Figure 7.1).

Simple recording sheets, for example, Figures 7.2, 7.3 and 7.4.

Figure 7.1 Using scientific equipment on a mini-beast hunt

Mini-beasts

Mini-beasts that crawl.

mini-beasts

Figure 7.2 'Mini-beasts that crawl' recording sheet

© Claire Marvin and Chris Stokoe (2003) *Access to Science*, David Fulton Publishers.

Mini-beasts

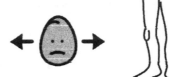

Mini-beasts with no legs.

mini-beasts

Figure 7.3 'Mini-beasts with no legs' recording sheet

© Claire Marvin and Chris Stokoe (2003) *Access to Science*, David Fulton Publishers.

Mini-beasts

Mini-beasts with legs and wings.

mini-beasts

Figure 7.4 'Mini-beasts with legs and wings' recording sheet

Song

(to the tune of 'She'll be coming round the mountain')

1. There's a tiny caterpillar on a leaf – wiggle, wiggle,
   There's a tiny caterpillar on a leaf – wiggle, wiggle,
   There's a tiny caterpillar, tiny caterpillar,
   Tiny caterpillar on a leaf – wiggle, wiggle,

Other verses

2. He will eat the leaves around him till he's full – munch, munch

3. A cocoon is what he's spinning for his home – spin, spin

4. Then he'll be a butterfly and fly away – flutter, flutter

5. Repeat all four actions, beginning:

   So that tiny caterpillar went like this – wiggle, wiggle, munch, munch, spin, spin, flutter, flutter

Skeletons

Funny Bones by Janet and Alan Ahlberg (1990) Heinemann, London.

Funny Bones (BBC video)

Camille Saint-Saëns *Carnival of the Animals* (Decca)

'Modroc' is available from educational supplies under the 'Art' section.

Song

(to the tune of 'Bobby Shaftoe')

I've got a skeleton in my body,
I've got a skeleton in my body,
I've got a skeleton in my body,
Bones I can feel but cannot see.

Verses

Make up verses by asking pupils to say in which body parts they can feel bones, e.g.

I've got bones in my shoulders and my knees,
I've got bones in my shoulders and my knees,
I've got bones in my shoulders and my knees,
Bones I can feel but cannot see.

CD-ROMs

The 3-D Body Adventure (Dorling Kindersley)

The Ultimate Human Body (Dorling Kindersley)

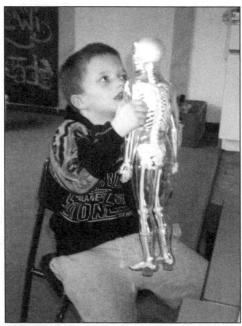

Figure 7.5 Interacting with the skeleton

Electricity

Awesome Experiments in Electricity and Magnetism by Michael Dispezio (1998) Sterling Publishing Co Inc., New York.

Useful website: www.schoolzone.co.uk

Milk shake

Ingredients

1 litre of milk
Selection of soft fruits, e.g. bananas, strawberries, kiwi fruits
4 scoops of soft vanilla ice cream

Equipment

Electric blender
Large switch
Chopping boards
Safety knives
Spoons
Glasses or cups

Method

Liquidise selected fruit to a purée and sieve to remove seeds. Rinse the blender and return purée and add 1 scoop of ice cream and add 250ml milk. Blend and pour into glasses or cups.

Popcorn

Microwave popcorn is available from most major supermarkets and comes with instructions for use.

Washing and drying

Mixing bicarbonate of soda and soap flakes will produce 'fizz'. Try colouring it with food colouring to add visual interest.

Simple recording sheet, for example, Figure 7.6.

Songs

1. (to the tune of 'Knees up Mother Brown')

   Wash the dirty clothes
   Wash the dirty clothes
   Scrub them this way, squeeze them that way,
   Wash the dirty clothes.

   Dry the clean wet clothes,
   Dry the clean wet clothes,
   Blow them this way, blow them that way,
   Dry the clean wet clothes.

2. (to the tune of 'In and out the dusky bluebells')

   In and out the clean wet washing,
   In and out the clean wet washing,
   In and out the clean wet washing,
   Can you feel it dripping?
   (Repeat verse to last line:)
   Can you smell it drying?

Washing

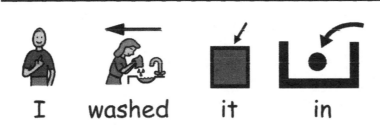

I   made   a   stain   on   fabric

I   washed   it   in

Now   it   is   _____

Figure 7.6 'Washing' recording sheet

© Claire Marvin and Chris Stokoe (2003) *Access to Science*, David Fulton Publishers.

CHAPTER EIGHT

Practical materials for Key Stage 3

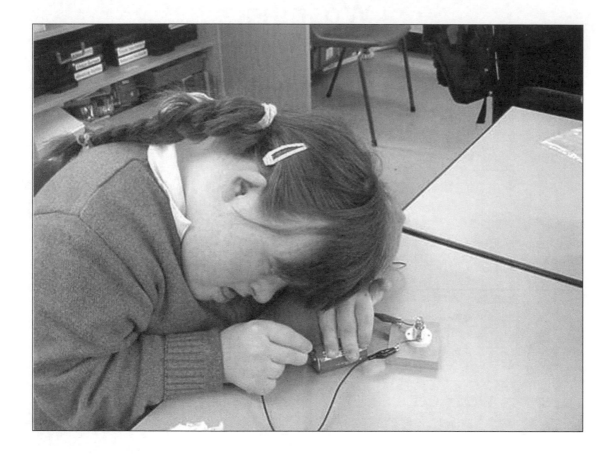

Experiences and opportunities at Key Stage 3

The focus of teaching science at Key Stage 3 may be on giving pupils opportunities to:

- consolidate and generalise existing knowledge, skills and understanding through first-hand experiences that link to their everyday lives, for example, about healthy lifestyle, insulation
- plan for and extend investigative activities with their peers taking more responsibility for their own learning and achievement in wider environments, for example, in a mainstream science laboratory.

Given these opportunities in science at Key Stage 3 the QCA/DfEE (2001a: 21) guidelines suggest that:

all pupils with learning difficulties (including those with the most profound disabilities)	extend their scientific experience and understanding through explorations, experiments and investigations appropriate for their age. They work with others to collect evidence.
most pupils with learning difficulties (including those with severe difficulties in learning) who will develop further skills, knowledge and understanding in most aspects of the subject	know they need to ask questions about how things work and can make suggestions about how to find answers and to solve problems. They use a range of observations and measurements and different modes of data collection. Pupils link their knowledge to their everyday lives, including their personal health and lifestyles. They use some reference sources; communicate what they have done; describe what has happened; draw conclusions from their data, and recognise when a test is largely fair or unfair.
a few pupils with learning difficulties who will develop further aspects of knowledge, skills and understanding in the subject	make comparisons and recognise significant differences when interpreting the results of tests and investigations. They communicate their ideas and findings. They understand some ways in which scientists work; evaluate their work; select and use reference sources and begin to apply their knowledge and understanding of scientific ideas to familiar phenomena and everyday things.

Learning opportunities at Key Stage 3

Tables 8.1–8.6 are examples of a subject leader's medium-term plans for science-focused units of work at Key Stage 3 covered over a term or half a term. These are followed by Table 8.7, an example of a class teacher's planning sheet for a series of weekly lessons from a selected unit of work, and Table 8.8, a short-term plan exemplifying a single session from within the series.

Table 8.1 Example of a subject leader's medium-term planning – Key Stage 3, Foundation, Sc3 Metals, non-metals and magnetism

Subject Leader's Medium-term Planning

Key Stage: 3 Foundation	Subject: Science	PoS: Sc3 Metals, non-metals and magnetism	Curriculum links: n/a	L-TP reference: Year 1 Spring 2
Intended learning outcomes	**Activities**		**Assessment prompts**	
Sc1: Scientific enquiry All pupils will encounter a range of scientific experiences and sensory resources linked to the programme of study. These opportunities will provide a context in which pupils learn to: • demonstrate emerging awareness **P1(ii)** • respond and show interest **P2(i)** • engage and explore indiscriminately **P2(ii)** • participate intentionally **P3(i)** • initiate involvement. **P3(ii)**	Introduce the PoS by exploring a selection of metal and non-metal spoons. Use pans, tins, washing bowls to experiment with different sounds. Compare metal-on-metal with metal-on-plastic and record pupils' likes and dislikes and encourage them to make choices and initiate actions. Place metal objects, e.g. jug, cutlery, kitchen utensils, within layers of fabrics and materials and encourage pupils to search for them. As the pupils locate the objects, explore their properties, e.g. cold, smooth, shiny. Repeat the activity using a selection of non-metal resources. Explore the properties of a variety of metallic materials, e.g. foil, space blanket, hologram paper. Listen to the sounds they make when crumpled or watch as they catch the light from a light beam. Use dried peas, lentils or gravel and place them in metal containers. Encourage the pupils to stir the materials with their hands or wooden and metal spoons. Listen to the different sounds they make and communicate preferences and dislikes.		Pupils may: • demonstrate simple reflex responses and be resistant or passive to supported sensory activities. *Example:* startling to the sound of a metal spoon banged on a saucepan or curling fingers around a magnetic rod. **P1(i)** • focus their attention briefly on people, objects and events, and give intermittent reactions. *Example:* accepting a fully supported exploration of metal resources or showing a fleeting interest in reflective surfaces of metal resources. **P1(ii)** • accept and engage in supported exploration and reject or begin to show interest in new and unfamiliar activities and resources. *Example:* tracking the movement of objects attracted to a large magnet or making percussive sounds with metal and wooden resources with support. **P2(i)**	

Intended learning outcomes	Activities	Assessment prompts
	Use a variety of commercial fridge magnets or produce their own using preferred images, e.g. pop stars, sports personalities, favourite foods, animals, or other topics of interest. Laminate the pictures and attach small magnets. Use magnetic boards to display them.	• interact with people and begin to explore objects proactively; perform actions through supported trial and error and communicate preferences and dislikes. *Example*: using their hands to stir dried peas in a metal container or reaching out to explore different fridge magnets on a magnetic whiteboard. **P2(ii)**
	Use a selection of familiar objects or personal items (e.g. standing frame) that have metal components. Experiment with different magnets, e.g. large horseshoe magnet, or rods. Experience feeling the magnetic force.	• begin to show interest in and observe the results of their actions; choose to interact with people actively, and explore objects with less support. *Example*: searching for metallic objects hidden within layers of fabric or crumpling foil or a space blanket and listening to the sounds they make. **P3(i)**
	Put steel ball bearings on a thin plastic or aluminium tray. Use a large magnet under the tray to make the balls move. Take turns to observe or initiate the movements. Mark out a track on the tray with tape or marker pen. Help the pupils to make the balls follow the track.

Test a selection of objects to discover which are magnetic. Make a large collage of a magnet and attach images of the objects tested. | • explore objects independently for short periods and initiate interactions with people; demonstrate an emerging potential to solve simple problems and begin to anticipate the outcomes of activities. *Example*: using a magnet to move iron filings within a closed frame or choosing and exploring the magnetic properties of personal or favourite resources. **P3(ii)** |
| | Play a magnetic fishing game to reinforce the concepts of object permanence and cause and effect. Alternatively use magnets and iron filings contained within commercially produced frames to make patterns. | |
| **Key words**
Metal   Magnet
Shiny   Dull
Stick   Pull | | |

107

Table 8.2 Example of a subject leader's medium-term planning – Key Stage 3, Access and Extension, Sc3 Metals, non-metals and magnetism

Subject Leader's Medium-term Planning

Key Stage: 3 Access & Extension	Subject: Science	PoS: Sc3 Metals, non-metals and magnetism	Curriculum links: ICT, Art and design	L-TP reference: Year 1 Spring 2
Intended learning outcomes	Activities		Assessment prompts	
Sc1: Scientific enquiry To develop skills of scientific enquiry through activities which provide opportunities to: • anticipate and make choices • use senses to investigate materials and resources • observe, comment and measure • record and evaluate. **Sc3: Materials and their properties** **Access** To test and group metallic and non-metallic materials. To test and group magnetic and non-magnetic metals.	Use a selection of everyday familiar objects, e.g. saucepan, wooden spoon, plastic jug. Sort into groups, i.e. classify by material type. Label each group, e.g. 'wood', 'plastic'. Present a selection of magnets, e.g. horseshoe, rod, investigate how many of the materials are magnetic. Go on a 'material hunt' around the classroom. Each pupil selects three objects to test for magnetic properties. Encourage pupils to predict which will be attracted to a magnet. Test each object with the magnet and group them into magnetic and non-magnetic sets. Take photographs for follow-up work. Make a fishing game. Use images of pupils' interests, e.g. pop stars, TV or computer game characters, to make into the 'fish'. Make fishing rods out of thin garden cane, string and magnets and play the game together, reinforcing the concept of turn-taking. Make fridge magnets using craft moulds and plaster of Paris. *Art and design link*		Pupils may: • handle or observe resources with curiosity and demonstrate a general interest in their properties, features and functions; imitate familiar actions; know that certain actions cause predictable results. *Example:* intentionally striking a saucepan with a wooden spoon or watching the movement of magnetic marbles towards a rod with interest. **P4** • focus on activities and anticipate actions; explore and group resources with support, and respond to simple scientific questions using their preferred method of communication. *Example:* anticipating their turn when playing a magnetic fishing game or recognising which objects were attracted to their magnets. **P5**	

Intended learning outcomes	Activities	Assessment prompts
Extension To know that sometimes magnets attract or repel each other.	Use magnetic rods and magnetic marbles of different colours. Give each pupil a rod and place the marbles onto a tray. Set a timer and ask the pupils to 'catch' as many of the same coloured marble within a time limit. Investigate everyday uses of magnets, e.g. children's games, door fastenings, notice-boards, fridge magnets, magnetic letters and numbers.	• recognise features of living things and objects; begin to generalise and predict outcomes, and explore resources intentionally and appropriately and group them to simple given criteria. *Example:* guessing which items would be attracted to their magnets or making independent selections of resources to test for magnetic properties. **P6**
	Play a game with magnets and paper clips. Predict how many paper clips each pupil will pick up with their magnets within a set time. Use a selection of metallic objects, e.g. paper clips and coins, and group them into magnetic and non-magnetic sets. Make an interactive 'science corner' using the tested resources for the pupils to investigate during their leisure time. Use computer graphics or picture symbols to create a pictorial record of familiar metallic and non-metallic objects. *ICT link*	• investigate resources purposefully and group them reliably; make observations and offer ideas using simple scientific language; begin to plan, record and evaluate their work with support. *Example:* gathering groups of shiny and dull metal objects to test for magnetic properties or recording that 'N' and 'S' magnets stick together. **P7**
Key words Metal Magnet Shiny Dull Stick Attract North South Repel	Hang a large single-pole horseshoe magnet (marked 'N' or 'S') on a string from the ceiling. Investigate magnets with like and unlike poles. Observe the difference in behaviour as the magnets either repel or attract. Video and watch the investigation. Comment on and record their findings.	• make independent contributions to enquiries and answer simple reasoning questions; recognise similarities and differences in the features of living things and properties of objects consistently. *Example:* giving an appropriate response to 'why' questions, e.g. 'Why did the paper clips stick to the magnet?' or recognising that 'N' and 'N' or 'S' and 'S' magnets do not attract. **P8** Refer to the National Curriculum guidance for science assessment prompts beyond P8.

Table 8.3 Example of a subject leader's medium-term planning – Key Stage 3, Foundation, Sc4 Light and dark, the Earth and beyond

Subject Leader's Medium-term Planning

Key Stage: 3 Foundation	Subject: Science	PoS: Sc4 Light and dark, the Earth and beyond	Curriculum links: Maths, English, ICT, PE	L-TP reference: Year 2 Autumn 2
Intended learning outcomes	Activities		Assessment prompts	
Sc1: Scientific enquiry All pupils will encounter a range of scientific experiences and sensory resources linked to the programme of study. These opportunities will provide a context in which pupils learn to: • demonstrate emerging awareness **P1(ii)** • respond and show interest **P2(i)** • engage and explore indiscriminately **P2(ii)** • participate intentionally **P3(i)** • initiate involvement. **P3(ii)**	Hide a range of remote-controlled or sound-activated light sources under translucent covers and encourage the pupils to search for them and explore their functions. Investigate a range of light sources; find out what makes them work and which they like best, e.g. disco lights. Record experiences on a simple worksheet using digital photographs. Encourage the pupils to explore and operate a variety of light sources in a darkened or multisensory area. Record their preferences or dislikes. *ICT link* Go outside and observe own shadow moving. Experience watching the different shadow shapes created by moving parts of their bodies. Use coloured tape to mark the shadow outlines so that they are visible to the pupils. Experience being in a 'blackout' – introduce different lights so that room gets brighter and brighter. Reinforce key words 'dark' and 'light', 'night' and 'day'.		Pupils may: • demonstrate simple reflex responses and be resistant or passive to supported sensory activities. *Example:* blinking rapidly when taken from a darkened room into the sunshine or startling when moved or rocked on a large PE ball. **P1(i)** • focus their attention briefly on people, objects and events, and give intermittent reactions. *Example:* showing fleeting interest in the patterns of disco lights or reacting to the darkening or lightening of a room. **P1(ii)** • accept and engage in supported exploration and reject or begin to show interest in new and unfamiliar activities and resources. *Example:* refusing to explore unfamiliar materials presented as 3-D models for planet work or showing interest in a specific light source. **P2(i)**	

Intended learning outcomes	Activities	Assessment prompts
	Use water sprays or a hosepipe outdoors in the sun. Observe the 'rainbow' as the water catches the light.	• interact with people and begin to explore objects proactively; perform actions through supported trial and error and communicate preferences and dislikes. *Example*: pressing a switch to operate a light source with support or watching the movement of light beams in a darkened room. **P2(ii)**
	Make 3-D planets, e.g. Saturn, Mars, the Earth – use 'round' balloons on which to build layers. Paint or cover with collage materials.	
	Make sun, moon and stars mobiles out of reflective materials or use stencils/stamps and metallic paints to create patterns or sequences. *Maths link*	• begin to show interest in and observe the results of their actions; choose to interact with people actively, and explore objects with less support. *Example*: reaching out to touch a planet mobile or exploring a favourite light source with minimal support. **P3(i)**
	Make silhouette images using an OHP. Cut out different sizes and encourage pupils to make a design of dark on light and/or the reverse.	
	Use a large PE ball, trampet (small trampoline) or blanket. Pupils experience moving to Holst's *The Planets* or *2001: A Space Odyssey* (opening of Richard Strauss's *Also Sprach Zarathustra*). Pupils experience circular movements. *PE link*	• explore objects independently for short periods and initiate interactions with people; demonstrate an emerging potential to solve simple problems and begin to anticipate the outcomes of activities. *Example*: searching for a concealed light source or observing the movement of patterns created by their own shadows. **P3(ii)**
	Make 'space' biscuits, for example stars and moons. Decorate with edible silver/gold leaf or icing. Alternatively use salt dough (see Resources at the end of the book) and paint them as Christmas decorations or to use as mobiles.	
Key words Sun Light Dark Night Day	Tell a sensory space story. Illustrate it with a range of resources, e.g. a mirror ball to simulate the moon. Encourage the pupils to explore the resources used to support the story and respond to the actions, e.g. being rocked in their chairs to simulate a moon landing. *English link*	

Table 8.4 Example of a subject leader's medium-term planning – Key Stage 3, Access and Extension, Sc4 Light and dark, the Earth and beyond

Subject Leader's Medium-term Planning

Key Stage: 3 Access & Extension	Subject: Science	PoS: Sc4 Light and dark, the Earth and beyond	Curriculum links: ICT, English, PE	L-TP reference: Year 2 Autumn 2
Intended learning outcomes	**Activities**		**Assessment prompts**	
Sc1: Scientific enquiry To develop skills of scientific enquiry through activities which provide opportunities to: • anticipate and make choices • use senses to investigate materials and resources • observe, comment and measure • record and evaluate.	Investigate a selection of light sources, e.g. torch, candle in a darkened room. Decide which gives the brightest light. Record the results. Use a globe in a darkened room. Shine a torch on it to represent the sun and observe how some parts are in the dark while others are visible. Research the differences between how the world looks at night and in the day. Use video clips, books and posters to promote discussion. Make a pictogram or write a diary recording the activities pupils experience routinely each day and night, or when it is light and dark.		Pupils may: • handle or observe resources with curiosity and demonstrate a general interest in their properties, features and functions; imitate familiar actions; know that certain actions cause predictable results. *Example:* becoming anxious in a darkened room or switching on a lamp to lighten a room. **P4** • focus on activities and anticipate actions; explore and group resources with support, and respond to simple scientific questions using their preferred method of communication. *Example:* giving an appropriate answer to the question: 'Is it light or dark?' or responding to pictures of the solar system in an atlas. **P5** • recognise features of living things and objects; begin to generalise and predict outcomes, and explore resources intentionally and appropriately and group them to simple given criteria. *Example:* sorting picture symbols of stars and moons or knowing that they can see the stars at night, not in the day. **P6**	
Sc4: Physical processes **Access** To distinguish between night and day (dark and light). To investigate a range of light sources and find out how they work. To know that it is light in the day and dark at night. To name 'Sun', 'Moon' and 'stars'.	Make a 'black box'. Stick shiny stars, moons inside; cut viewing and light holes. Test what happens when the light hole is covered, or extra light is added. Use the Internet and/or visit the library to find out about the Earth and beyond. Focus on the Earth, Sun, Moon and stars. *ICT link*			

Intended learning outcomes	Activities	Assessment prompts
Extension To identify the Sun as a natural light source.	Plan a visit to a planetarium or invite a mobile one to school. Experience looking at the solar system. Follow-up work: make tactile images of star constellations on a black sky or individual ones as dot-to-dot patterns. Select two or three planets to research. Make a class book or fact sheets. Read *Blast Off* together. Make 3-D rockets: role-play a space journey; make costumes/space helmets. Use *2001: A Space Odyssey* music (opening of Richard Strauss's *Also Sprach Zarathustra*) or Holst's *The Planets* to choreograph a dance piece. *English & PE links* Write poems or space stories and act them out to reinforce key words and concepts. *English link* Investigate 'fact' and 'fiction' aspects of the Earth and beyond. Watch extracts of *Star Wars* or *Star Trek* and compare to video footage of real space travel. Discuss the possibility of aliens. Design their own space being and write a profile for it, e.g. planet origin, what it eats. *English link*	• investigate resources purposefully and group them reliably; make observations and offer ideas using simple scientific language; begin to plan, record and evaluate their work with support. *Example:* making a symbolic record of artificial light sources or deciding which light source provided the best light in a darkened environment. **P7** • make independent contributions to enquiries and answer simple reasoning questions; recognise similarities and differences in the features of living things and properties of objects consistently. *Example:* naming activities carried out during the day and at night or looking at different images of planets such as Saturn, Mars and the Earth and describing their differences. **P8** Refer to the National Curriculum guidance for science assessment prompts beyond P8.

Key words

Sun — Light
Dark — Night
Day — Planet
Moon — Stars
Space — Earth

Table 8.5 Example of a subject leader's medium-term planning – Key Stage 3, Foundation, Sc2 Nutrition and dental care

Subject Leader's Medium-term Planning

Key Stage: 3 Foundation	Subject: Science	PoS: Sc2 Nutrition and dental care	Curriculum links: PSHE, ICT	L-TP reference: Year 3 Autumn 1
Intended learning outcomes		**Activities**	**Assessment prompts**	
Sc1: Scientific enquiry All pupils will encounter a range of scientific experiences and sensory resources linked to the programme of study. These opportunities will provide a context in which pupils learn to:		Introduce the PoS by exploring a variety of fresh fruits. Use soft fruits, e.g. bananas, pears, plums, encourage the pupils to taste and smell them and to feel the different textures. Keep a record of preferences and dislikes. Use computer graphics to make a personal record, e.g. 'All about me'. *PSHE link*	Pupils may: • demonstrate simple reflex responses and be resistant or passive to supported sensory activities. *Example*: recoiling from the feel of a toothbrush on their lips or experiencing a visit to a greengrocer's shop. **P1(i)**	
• demonstrate emerging awareness **P1(ii)** • respond and show interest **P2(i)**		Use baking apples, peel them and taste them raw. Cook them in the microwave, taste with and without sugar. Which do pupils prefer? Use a large switch to operate the microwave or encourage the pupils to press the start button and listen for the 'finishing noise'. *ICT link*	• focus their attention briefly on people, objects and events, and give intermittent reactions. *Example*: listening to the sound of a microwave or reacting to the taste of a baking apple. **P1(ii)**	
• engage and explore indiscriminately **P2(ii)** • participate intentionally **P3(i)** • initiate involvement. **P3(ii)**		Use a juicing machine to make a vegetable and a fruit juice, e.g. carrot, tomato, orange. Use large switches to operate the machine. Taste both and record preferences or dislikes. Take photographs of pupils making and tasting for their personal records. *PSHE link* Write to parents and request a list of favourite foods. Make a poster using pupils' photographs and computer graphics of their favourite foods. Make an 'I like' list for their personal records. *PSHE link*	• accept and engage in supported exploration and reject or begin to show interest in new and unfamiliar activities and resources. *Example*: demonstrating a preference for the taste of banana milk shake or exploring the properties of soft fruits with support. **P2(i)**	

Intended learning outcomes	Activities	Assessment prompts
	Visit a greengrocer's, look and feel the different fruits and vegetables available. Encourage the pupils to look for specific items. Take photographs of the visit for follow-up work.	• interact with people and begin to explore objects proactively; perform actions through supported trial and error and communicate preferences and dislikes. **P2(ii)** *Example:* actively exploring teeth cleaning resources using different senses or pressing a switch with support to operate a juicing machine.
	Taste chocolate, i.e. milk, white and plain, encourage the pupils to look at their teeth in the mirror after eating. Help them to clean their teeth. Use different toothbrushes, e.g. soft bristles, electric, and toothpastes, let the pupils choose. Take photographs of 'before' and 'after'.	• begin to show interest in and observe the results of their actions; choose to interact with people actively, and explore objects with less support. **P3(i)** *Example:* communicating a preference for banana purée or exploring the properties of junk food packaging.
	Arrange for the pupils to bring in a toothbrush. Develop pupils' tolerance to having their teeth cleaned, and encourage them to learn how to clean their teeth independently. *PSHE link*	• explore objects independently for short periods and initiate interactions with people; demonstrate an emerging potential to solve simple problems and begin to anticipate the outcomes of activities. **P3(ii)** *Example:* attempting to open the packaging of a favourite food item or watching the action of a juicing machine.
Key words Teeth Food Taste Clean		

115

Table 8.6 Example of a subject leader's medium-term planning – Key Stage 3, Access and Extension, Sc2 Nutrition and dental care

Subject Leader's Medium-term Planning

Key Stage: 3 Access & Extension	Subject: Science	PoS: Sc2 Nutrition and dental care	Curriculum links: ICT, DT, PSHE	L-TP reference: Year 3 Autumn 1
Intended learning outcomes		Activities	Assessment prompts	
Sc1: Scientific enquiry To develop skills of scientific enquiry through activities which provide opportunities to:		Using supermarket catalogues and magazines, cut out pictures of different food groups to classify and make posters. Use the local or school library to research basic food groups.	Pupils may:	
• anticipate and make choices • use senses to investigate materials and resources • observe, comment and measure • record and evaluate.		Discuss the different food groups (use posters as a visual aid) and their benefits to particular parts of the body, e.g. milk/calcium for healthy bones and teeth. Plan a healthy snack that is nutritionally balanced. Use a computer graphics program to make a menu or shopping list. *ICT link*	• handle or observe resources with curiosity and demonstrate a general interest in their properties, features and functions; imitate familiar actions; know that certain actions cause predictable results. *Example:* communicating a dislike for raw carrot or imitating teeth cleaning actions. **P4**	
Sc2: Life and living processes **Access** To learn to communicate their preferences and dislikes for different foods.		Shop for, prepare and present the healthy snack. Take photographs, then share the meal. Make a chart of what was liked best, and disliked most. Evaluate the meal and discuss what the pupils would change. *DT link*	• focus on activities and anticipate actions; explore and group resources with support, and respond to simple scientific questions using their preferred method of communication. *Example:* sorting familiar food packaging, e.g. egg boxes, yoghurt pots, or being able to recognise a carrot in a group of vegetables. **P5**	
To know the importance of regularly cleaning their teeth. To distinguish between 'healthy' and 'junk' foods.		Keep a record of food eaten over a three-day period (this could be homework). Compare the quantities of 'junk' food and 'healthy' food eaten. Use picture symbols to make a chart with 'junk' on one side and 'healthy' on the other. *PSHE link*	• recognise features of living things and objects; begin to generalise and predict outcomes, and explore resources intentionally and appropriately and group them to simple given criteria. *Example:* grouping fruits and vegetables or predicting that chocolate will stick to their teeth. **P6**	

Intended learning outcomes	Activities	Assessment prompts
Extension To know that a balanced diet helps them to be healthy. To know that not cleaning their teeth can lead to tooth decay.	Taste and compare 'healthy' and 'junk' foods and record their preferences and dislikes using picture symbols or computer graphics. *ICT link* Construct a 3-D diet display of balance scales using objects relating to 'junk' food such as cola cans, burger boxes on one side and objects relating to 'healthy' foods such as egg boxes and milk cartons on the other. Make a full-sized body outline and stick pictures or computer graphics of foods that help different body parts stay healthy. Invite the dental hygienist to talk to the pupils about oral hygiene. Video or photograph the session for follow-up work. Discuss which food group the pupils think is most harmful to teeth. Eat chocolate, look at pupils' teeth before and afterwards using a magnifying mirror. Clean teeth, then use mirror to check if the chocolate or sweet stains have gone. Take digital photographs to make a pictorial sequence of the teeth-cleaning method. Repeat the experiment but use 'healthy' foods, e.g. celery, raw carrot. Ask pupils to look at their teeth in the mirror, do the foods leave a residue? Use dental floss to see if any food remains between the teeth. Photograph the investigation. Use photographs from previous lessons to compare results. Design and make a poster of foods that are not as harmful to teeth as sweets.	• investigate resources purposefully and group them reliably; make observations and offer ideas using simple scientific language; begin to plan, record and evaluate their work with support. *Example:* grouping specific dairy products, e.g. cheese, yoghurt, milk, or evaluating which foods are best for healthy teeth. **P7** • make independent contributions to enquiries and answer simple reasoning questions; recognise similarities and differences in the features of living things and properties of objects consistently. *Example:* finding books in the library relating to oral hygiene or making an appropriate contribution to the planning of a healthy snack menu. **P8** Refer to the National Curriculum guidance for science assessment prompts beyond P8.
Key words Teeth Diet Healthy Clean Food		

Table 8.7 Example of a class teacher's medium-term planning – Key Stage 3

Class Teacher's Medium-term Planning

Subject: Science			PoS: Sc3 Metals, non-metals and magnetism
Class: Senior 2		Teacher: Chris	Long-term plan ref.: Year 1, Spring 2
Lesson	ILO (F)*	Focus skills (A–E)	Activities *(Three-part lesson)*
1	*All pupils encounter and have access to a broad range of sensory experiences and activities presented in a scientific context through which they may demonstrate awareness; respond and show interest; engage and explore indiscriminately; participate intentionally, and initiate involvement.*	**Sc1 skill:** Sorting **Key skill:** Problem solving	Introduction: music cue; key words/symbols. Sort non-metals/metals; test with magnets. Regroup them into magnetic/non-magnetic sets. Plenary: recap key words and discuss object groups.
2		**Sc1 skill:** Predicting **Key skill:** Problem solving	Introduction: music cue; key words/symbols. Material hunt: select three times per pupil. Predict and test the magnetic properties. Plenary: recap key words; present own findings.
3		**Sc1 skill:** Planning **Key skill:** Improving own learning	Introduction: music cue; key words/symbols. Make fridge magnets out of plaster or clay. Plenary: show work and plan next step.
4		**Sc1 skill:** Testing **Key skill:** Problem solving	Introduction: music cue; key words/symbols. Complete fridge magnets, i.e. paint/decorate. Plenary: show work and test effectiveness.
5		**Sc1 skill:** Recording **Key skill:** Improving own learning	Introduction: music cue; key words/symbols. Test magnetic properties of common objects, e.g. drink cans, cutlery, paper clips. Record findings. Plenary: discuss magnetic items discovered.
6		**Sc1 skill:** Evaluating **Key skill:** Problem solving	Introduction: music cue; key words/symbols. Make magnetic fishing game – use laminated pictures of favourite TV/pop stars. Make rods with magnets. Plenary: evaluate which game worked the best.
7		**Sc1 skill:** Problem solving **Key skill:** Working with others	**Assessment** Free-choice activities: exploring magnets and materials; magnetic construction; fishing games. One-to-one observation of pupils' knowledge/skills.

Science learning outcomes	Cross-curricular links	Key words
To distinguish between metals and non-metals. To group magnetic and non-magnetic objects. To describe the behaviour of magnets and metals.	Art and design	• Metal • Shiny • Magnet • Dull • Pull • Stick

*ILO(F): Intended learning outcomes (Foundation)

Table 8.8 Example of short-term planning – Key Stage 3

Short-term planning

Subject: Science	PoS: Sc3 Metals, non-metals and magnetism	Date: 7th Feb.
Cross-curricular links: n/a		**Class:** Senior 2

Intended learning outcomes (*Including key skills*)	Key words
Foundation (P1–3) To develop communication and problem-solving skills. To develop cooperative work skills. To be proactive in their exploration of resources. **Access (P4–7)** To develop understanding of cause and effect. To recognise simple properties of metal objects. To explore the magnetic properties of resources actively. **Extension (P8–NC1/2)** To know tht some metal objects/materials will stick to a magnet and others with not.	• Magnet • Metal • Stick • Pull • Shiny • Dull

Activities (*Include differentiation for pupils at Foundation, Access and Extension*)

Introduction: music cue, key words and symbols. Use large horseshoe magnet as object of reference and ask pupils to guess which resources will be attracted. Test them out.
Split into groups.

Group 1 (Foundation)
Explore properties of metallic resources, e.g. saucepans, spoons, tins. Bang, shake and rattle them. Use a large horseshoe magnet to attract objects.

Group 2 and 3 (Access & Extension)
Pupils investigate the properties of resources; predict magnetic behaviour. Record results on worksheet: cut and stick symbols.

Plenary: whole group. Show work and sets of objects. Recap key words.

Classroom organisation

Group 1	Lewis, Stacey and David	Staff	Paul and Sue
Group 2	Debbie, Peter and James	Staff	Margaret
Group 3	Natalie, Andrew, Shawn and Louise	Staff	Janet

Resources	IEP targets	
• Magnets: rods, horseshoes • Common metal objects: cans, paper clips, cutlery, saucepans • Recording sheet and symbols	**Debbie** **Lewis** **Natalie**	to wait calmly for her turn during a group activity. to accept coactive sensory exploration. to name her work independently.

Resource list for Key Stage 3

Metals, non-metals and magnetism

Electricity and Magnetism by Michael Dispezio (1998) Sterling Publishing Co. Inc., New York.

Useful websites: www.schoolzone.co.uk

Magnetic construction kits are available from most educational suppliers of primary resources.

Fishing game: use pictures of favourite characters or people, e.g. 'The Simpsons'. Cut out and stick onto card. Laminate them, punch a hole and thread a paperclip through. Make the rods out of thin garden sticks. Tie string onto one end of the stick and a small horseshoe magnet onto the other end of the string. Play the game. Make up rules.

A simple recording sheet, for example, Figure 8.1

Additional ideas

Crush iron-enriched cereal, e.g. Rice Crispies, into a powder. Sprinkle onto black paper. Slide a rod magnet underneath the paper and move it to create patterns with the powder.

Use magnetic letters and boards to form words that describe the behaviour of magnetic materials, e.g. 'pull', 'stick'.

Light and dark, the Earth and beyond

Gustav Holst *The Planets/Suite de Ballet* Op. 10 (Naxos)

Richard Strauss *Also Sprach Zarathustra* (Naxos)

Useful websites:

www.calacademy.org/research/library/biodiv/biblio/kidsastro.htm

www.planet-science.com

Simple recording sheets, for example, Figures 8.2 and 8.3.

Science fiction and fantasy videos, e.g. *2001: A Space Odyssey*, *Star Wars* and the *Star Trek* series are all available to purchase from Amazon.com. The website address is: www.amazon.com (click on the 'video' link, then on 'science fiction and fantasy'). This site also gives details of many other space-themed films that have suitable ratings for viewing in school.

Blast Off by Maryann Dobeck and Jamie Hogan (1998) Ginn, Aylesbury, Bucks.

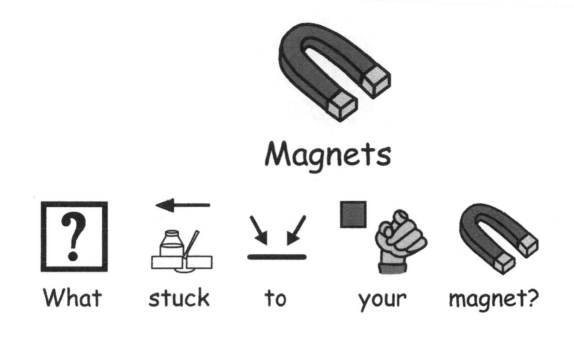

Magnets

What   stuck   to   your   magnet?

metals   and   magnets

Figure 8.1 'Magnets' recording sheet

Night

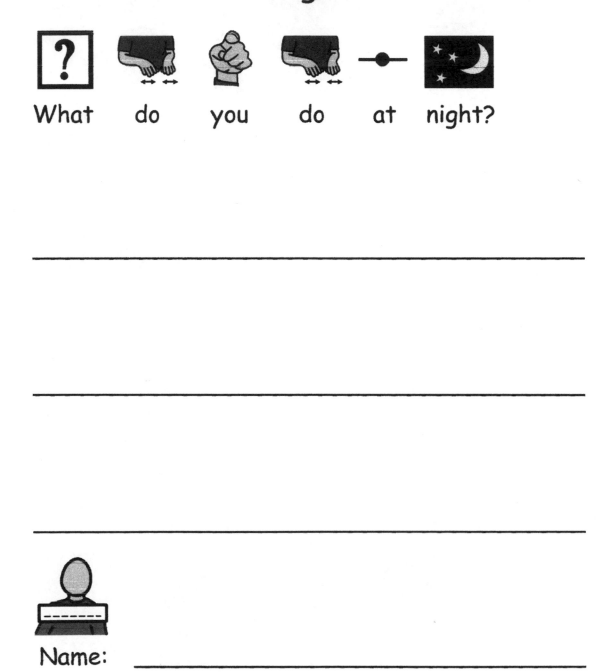

What   do   you   do   at   night?

_____

_____

_____

Name: _____

Figure 8.2 'Night' recording sheet

© Claire Marvin and Chris Stokoe (2003) *Access to Science*, David Fulton Publishers.

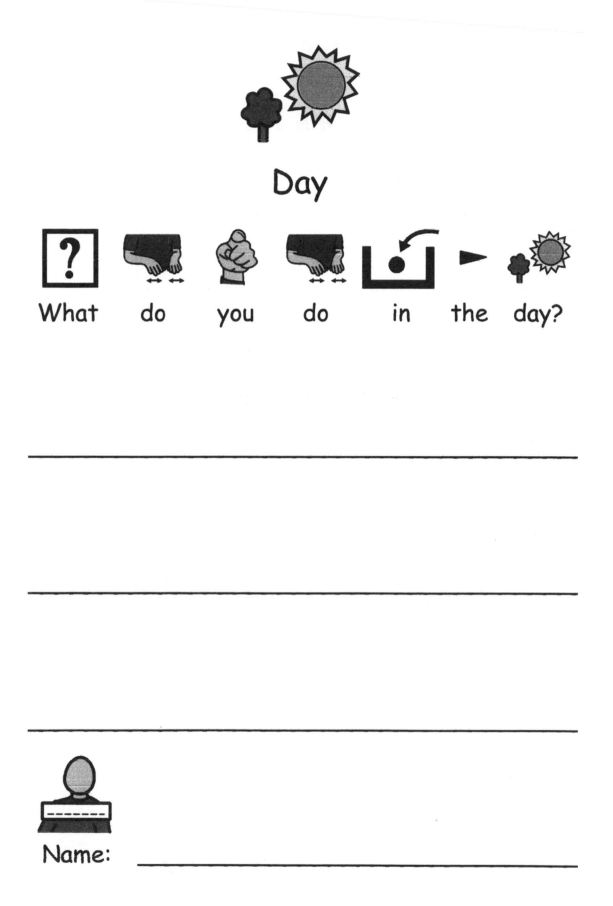

Day

What do you do in the day?

_____

_____

_____

Name: _____

Figure 8.3 'Day' recording sheet

CHAPTER NINE
Practical materials for Key Stage 4

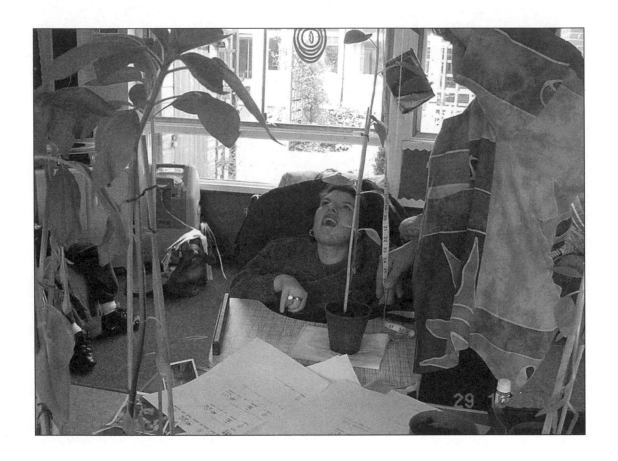

Experiences and opportunities at Key Stage 4

The focus of teaching science at Key Stage 4 may be on giving pupils opportunities to:

- continue to make links between acquired knowledge, skills and understanding and life experiences in appropriate learning environments, for example, college, community settings
- independently explore and participate in self-selected activities and investigations which encourage reflection on things around them, their bodies and their experiences.

Given these opportunities in science at Key Stage 4 the QCA/DfEE (2001a: 26) guidelines suggest that:

all pupils with learning difficulties (including those with the most profound disabilities)	use experience, knowledge, skills and understanding attained at earlier key stages to help them engage in new activities and investigations. Staff may need to support them in the use of a wide range of equipment and materials.
most pupils with learning difficulties (including those with severe difficulties in learning) who will develop further skills, knowledge and understanding in most aspects of the subject	make links between scientific experience and their everyday lives. They use different ways of presenting their data, *for example, charts, diagrams and drawings*. They recognise some relevant evidence, make simple evaluations of their work, and ask some scientific questions.
a few pupils with learning difficulties who will develop further aspects of knowledge, skills and understanding in the subject	understand some positive and negative effects of scientific and technological developments. They select and use appropriate reference sources. They carry out more systematic investigations, make more systematic observations and measurements, and apply their scientific knowledge to new situations.

Learning opportunities at Key Stage 4

Tables 9.1–9.4 are examples of a subject leader's medium-term plans for science-focused units of work at Key Stage 4 covered over a term or half a term. These are followed by Table 9.5, an example of a class teacher's planning sheet for a series of weekly lessons from a selected unit of work, and Table 9.6, a short-term plan exemplifying a single session from within the series.

Table 9.1 Example of a subject leader's medium-term planning – Key Stage 4, Foundation, Sc2 Horticulture

Subject Leader's Medium-term Planning

Key Stage: 4 Foundation	Subject: Science	PoS: Sc2 Horticulture	Accreditation: 5B ASDAN bronze	L-TP reference: Year 1 Summer 1
Intended learning outcomes	**Activities**		**Assessment prompts**	
Sc1: Scientific enquiry All pupils will encounter a range of scientific experiences and sensory resources linked to the programme of study. These opportunities will provide a context in which pupils learn to:	Introduce the PoS by exploring a variety of common garden resources, e.g. seeds, soil, compost and garden tools.		Pupils may:	
	Experience a visit to a garden centre. Use their senses to explore a variety of plants, e.g. herbs, fruit trees. Video the visit or use a digital camera to play back to pupils and facilitate follow-up work.		• demonstrate simple reflex responses and be resistant or passive to supported sensory activities. *Example:* making involuntary body movements when their hands are placed in compost or remaining passively alert during a visit to a garden centre. **P1(i)**	
• demonstrate emerging awareness **P1(ii)** • respond and show interest **P2(i)**	Visit a greengrocer's or supermarket. Choose different soft fruits and vegetables to purchase and take back to school.		• focus their attention briefly on people, objects and events, and give intermittent reactions. *Example:* accepting the touch or smell of a variety of herbs or glancing at the displays of fruits and vegetables in a supermarket. **P1(ii)**	
• engage and explore indiscriminately **P2(ii)** • participate intentionally **P3(i)**	Taste a variety of soft fruits, e.g. strawberries, bananas. Record pupils' preferences and dislikes. Make a pictogram of favourites, or include in personal profiles under 'likes and dislikes'.		• accept and engage in supported exploration and reject or begin to show interest in new and unfamiliar activities and resources. *Example:* showing pleasure when smelling a banana or accepting supported exploration of wet compost and seeds. **P2(i)**	
• initiate involvement. **P3(ii)**	Use fruits and vegetables to make patterns and prints with paints and inks.			
	Use their senses to compare fresh and tinned fruits (liquidised if necessary). Record pupils' responses.			

Intended learning outcomes	Activities	Assessment prompts
	Use fresh soft fruits to make 'smoothies'. Encourage the pupils to taste the different ingredients and make choices. Use their preferred ingredients to make smoothies in an electric blender; use large switches to operate it.	• interact with people and begin to explore objects proactively; perform actions through supported trial and error and communicate preferences and dislikes. *Example:* reaching out to explore the properties of a strawberry, e.g. tasting and smelling, or communicating dislike for the taste of lemon. **P2(ii)**
	Plant a pot with aromatic plants, e.g. herbs and lavender, to create a miniature sensory garden.	
	Make lavender bags or pillows for pupils to use during their leisure time.	• begin to show interest in and observe the results of their actions; choose to interact with people actively, and explore objects with less support.
	Use large magnifying glasses to look at different plants and explore their properties.	*Example:* making random print patterns with a halved pattern or actively exploring a fruit or vegetable hidden in a feely-box. **P3(i)**
	Place a fruit or vegetable into a 'feely-box'. Encourage the pupils to explore the contents. Present a choice of fruits and vegetables; match these to the unseen contents of the feely-box. Reveal contents of box, and see if they correspond.	• explore objects independently for short periods and initiate interactions with people; demonstrate an emerging potential to solve simple problems and begin to anticipate the outcomes of activities.
	Use natural dyes, e.g. red onion skins, turmeric, to make tie-dye patterns on an old plain T-shirt. Take photographs of the before and after states of the garments and of the pupils wearing them.	*Example:* working out how to transfer smoothies from a blender into a cup, e.g. spoon or pour, or filling and emptying plant pots with wet and dry compost. **P3(ii)**
Key words Feel Look Taste Smell Fruit Vegetable Plant	Produce a personal 'menu' of preferred plants, e.g. favourite colour of flower, taste of fruit, smell. Include the information in their personal profiles.	

Table 9.2 Example of a subject leader's medium-term planning – Key Stage 4, Access and Extension, Sc2 Horticulture

Subject Leader's Medium-term Planning

Key Stage: 4 Access & Extension	Subject: Science	PoS: Sc2 Horticulture	Accreditation: 5B ASDAN bronze	L-TP reference: Year 1 Summer 1
Intended learning outcomes		Activities	Assessment prompts	
Sc1: Scientific enquiry To develop skills of scientific enquiry through activities which provide opportunities to: • anticipate and make choices • use senses to investigate materials and resources • observe, comment and measure • record and evaluate. **Sc2: Life processes and living things** *Access* To identify and name common plant parts. To know the basic requirements to sustain plant life. To know that some plants are edible and some are not.		Plan a simple small or miniature garden. Identify a plot in the school grounds or decide on a container to use. Visit a garden centre to research ideas for the garden. Arrange for pupils to talk to one of the nursery workers about what they will need to care for the plants. Use video to record interview. Go to the library and borrow books about gardening. Use the Internet to gather information about plants and how to care for them. Write to local nurseries and parents/carers requesting donations of plants (these could be from the home garden). Discuss appropriate clothing for gardening, use catalogue pictures to record their ideas. Prepare plot for miniature garden. Use compost and peat mixed with soil, mark out areas with gravel or bark, and plant. Wear appropriate clothes. Make a rota of which pupils will be responsible for caring for the garden (Figure 9.1), on a daily or weekly basis. Produce a fact sheet to remind pupils of the routine care requirements.	Pupils may: • handle or observe resources with curiosity and demonstrate a general interest in their properties, features and functions; imitate familiar actions; know that certain actions cause predictable results. *Example:* actively exploring the properties of seeds in a tray or showing interest in online images of different flowering plants. **P4** • focus on activities and anticipate actions; explore and group resources with support, and respond to simple scientific questions using their preferred method of communication. *Example:* grouping common vegetables, e.g. carrots, potatoes, or pointing to a red flower on request. **P5** • recognise features of living things and objects; begin to generalise and predict outcomes, and explore resources intentionally and appropriately and group them to simple given criteria. *Example:* predicting that a white carnation will turn blue when placed in blue water or pointing to a yellow flower on request. **P6**	

Intended learning outcomes	Activities	Assessment prompts
Extension To classify edible and non-edible plants. To use secondary sources to find out how to grow plants from seed.	Use white flowers, e.g. carnations, and place them individually in water with different food colourings. Observe what happens to the colour of the petals and record the results. Try splitting the stems and placing each half in different coloured water. Take before and after photographs and evaluate the results. Research plants that can be grown in class from seed, e.g. sunflowers. Use the library or the Internet. Buy the seeds and grow them. Predict which plant will grow the tallest, or grow the most flowers. Record the growth, e.g. photograph different stages, and measure their height. Make and design posters to illustrate edible and non-edible plant groups. Plan a healthy snack using fruit and vegetables. Visit a farm shop or organic grower to purchase them. Prepare the snack for a specific event, e.g. a picnic or party.	• investigate resources purposefully and group them reliably; make observations and offer ideas using simple scientific language; begin to plan, record and evaluate their work with support. *Example:* recognising which sunflower has grown the tallest and measuring them to check or producing a list of basic resources and conditions needed to grow mushrooms. **P7** • make independent contributions to enquiries and answer simple reasoning questions; recognise similarities and differences in the features of living things and properties of objects consistently. *Example:* using their own simple criteria to group edible and non-edible plants or describing the similarities between green plants that are edible or non-edible. **P8**
Key words Plant Stem Leaf Flower Roots Food Light Water Sun Grow Garden Seeds Fruit Vegetable	Grow edible plants, e.g. cress, bean sprouts, mushrooms in a grow bag. Grow some in the dark and some in the light; record the results. Decide which ones will be best to eat. Make large posters illustrating the different parts of a plant, i.e. roots, stem, leaves, flower or fruit, and how to care for them.	Refer to the National Curriculum guidance for science assessment prompts beyond P8.

Table 9.3 Example of a subject leader's medium-term planning – Key Stage 4, Foundation, Sc4 Sound

Subject Leader's Medium-term Planning

Key Stage: 4 Foundation	Subject: Science	PoS: Sc4 Sound	Accreditation: n/a	L-TP reference: Year 2 Autumn 1
Intended learning outcomes	Activities		Assessment prompts	
Sc1: Scientific enquiry All pupils will encounter a range of scientific experiences and sensory resources linked to the programme of study. These opportunities will provide a context in which pupils learn to: • demonstrate emerging awareness **P1(ii)** • respond and show interest **P2(i)** • engage and explore indiscriminately **P2(ii)** • participate intentionally **P3(i)** • initiate involvement. **P3(ii)**	Introduce the PoS by listening to obvious contrasts in sound, i.e. loud sounds and silence. Practise not making any sound. Make a pattern using noise-makers or voice and then being silent. Record the pattern and use large switches to play back the composition. Hide battery-operated noise-makers under blankets or in a feely-bag. Encourage the pupils to listen and search for them. Sit the pupils 3 metres away from you. Walk slowly towards them singing or saying their names. Vary pitch and style of voice to add interest and encourage the pupils to look at you. Involve peer partners in the activity. Use a large screen and project voices from behind it. Encourage the pupils to listen and match the voice to a person or photographic image. Repeat the same activity but use familiar objects, e.g. favourite noise-makers, hair dryer. Use a resonance board to allow pupils to feel vibrations made with hands, feet or beaters. Record their preferences or dislikes.		Pupils may: • demonstrate simple reflex responses and be resistant or passive to supported sensory activities. *Example:* starting to the sound of beaters on a resonance board or becoming resistant when encouraged to feel a percussion instrument. **P1(i)** • focus their attention briefly on people, objects and events, and give intermittent reactions. *Example:* turning their head towards the sound of their name called from behind a screen or eye blinking when a preferred percussion instrument is played. **P1(ii)** • accept and engage in supported exploration and reject or begin to show interest in new and unfamiliar activities and resources. *Example:* giving brief eye contact when a familiar adult or peer moves towards them singing their name or listening to whale song. **P2(i)**	

Intended learning outcomes	Activities	Assessment prompts
	Use switches to operate a CD player. Select a variety of musical styles; listen to extracts and record pupils' favourites. Encourage them to turn the player on and off.	• interact with people and begin to explore objects proactively; perform actions through supported trial and error and communicate preferences and dislikes. **P2(ii)** *Example:* visually tracking the sound of a noise-maker played around their bodies or smiling in response to their name called in a high pitch.
	Listen to tapes of animal sounds and bird song, reinforced with objects of reference or pictures, e.g. feathers, picture of a blackbird. Record which sounds the pupils responded to.	
	Use a Soundbeam to create and compose sounds with involuntary or intentional body movements. Video the pupils engaging in the activity and play it back to them.	• begin to show interest in and observe the results of their actions; choose to interact with people actively, and explore objects with less support. **P3(i)** *Example:* gesturing towards a noise-maker to indicate a preference or searching for a battery-operated sound source hidden under a blanket or in a box.
	Attach small percussion instruments to pupils' hands or feet, or on hats and gloves. Encourage them to make intentional sounds.	
	Take turns to play different drums to create a pattern or musical dialogue.	• explore objects independently for short periods and initiate interactions with people; demonstrate an emerging potential to solve simple problems and begin to anticipate the outcomes of activities. **P3(ii)** *Example:* taking turns to bang a drum or making intentional movements to create sounds with a sound beam.
	Play preferred noise-makers, e.g. ocean drum, rain-stick, around the periphery of the pupils' bodies. Encourage them to follow the sound as it travels around them.	
	Use a voice distorter, e.g. karaoke machine. Amplify pupils' voices or vocalisations. Alter the pitch or tone and play back to the pupils.	
	Create a dark space; make different sounds with familiar objects. Encourage the pupils to identify the source when the light is turned on.	
Key words Loud Silent Noise Listen Hear Voice	Listen to sounds in and out of doors; make a pictogram of the ones they hear or identify, e.g. singing in assembly, sound of a car.	

Table 9.4 Example of a subject leader's medium-term planning – Key Stage 4, Access and Extension, Sc4 Sound

Subject Leader's Medium-term Planning

Key Stage: 4 Access & Extension	Subject: Science	PoS: Sc4 Sound	Accreditation: n/a	L-TP reference: Year 2 Autumn 1
Intended learning outcomes	Activities		Assessment prompts	
Sc1: Scientific enquiry To develop skills of scientific enquiry through activities which provide opportunities to: • anticipate and make choices • use senses to investigate materials and resources • observe, comment and measure • record and evaluate.	Contrast silence and sound. Use their voices or bodies to produce different sounds and compose a sound/silence pattern. Do the same using percussion instruments, e.g. vibraslap, large drum. Investigate ways of creating sounds using their own voice. Feel the vibrations as they blow or hum against their hands or arms. Use flexible card of different sizes and thickness and wave them to create sounds. Find out which makes the loudest and quietest sounds.		Pupils may: • handle or observe resources with curiosity and demonstrate a general interest in their properties, features and functions; imitate familiar actions; know that certain actions cause predictable results. *Example:* stamping their feet to create a loud sound or smiling in anticipation of a drumbeat. **P4** • focus on activities and anticipate actions; explore and group resources with support, and respond to simple scientific questions using their preferred method of communication. *Example:* grouping percussion instruments into sets of those you shake and those you beat or staying silent within a specified time frame. **P5**	
Sc4: Physical processes *Access* To investigate ways of producing sounds using their own bodies, objects or instruments. To know that they hear sounds. To recognise patterns of sound and silence.	Investigate materials and objects they can use to create sounds and vibrations they can hear, see and feel, e.g. tissue paper placed over a comb and blown through, or a ruler placed on the edge of a table and struck. Find out which resource makes the loudest and quietest sound. Use digital photographs or picture symbols to record their findings. Investigate different ways of projecting voices across the playground. Compare the different methods tried, e.g. using cupped hands, cardboard cone as a megaphone. Predict which will be the most effective; record and evaluate the methods used and check the accuracy of their predictions.		• recognise features of living things and objects; begin to generalise and predict outcomes, and explore resources intentionally and appropriately and group them to simple given criteria. *Example:* predicting that a drum will make a louder sound than a triangle or selecting appropriate materials to make a percussion instrument. **P6**	

Intended learning outcomes	Activities	Assessment prompts
Extension To know that vibrations produce sounds.	Present a selection of musical instruments and encourage the pupils to find out how they work. Observe the vibrations as they are played, e.g. strings on a guitar, gong. Create posters to show how different instruments work, e.g. pluck, strike.	• investigate resources purposefully and group them reliably; make observations and offer ideas using simple scientific language; begin to plan, record and evaluate their work with support. *Example:* recognising that their voice travelled further when using a megaphone or evaluating the effectiveness of a walkie-talkie compared to a mobile phone. **P7**
	Design own instruments, e.g. kazoo using a flattened kitchen roll tube with cellophane placed over a hole cut out of the top or drum using food wrap stretched over a plastic bucket. Investigate ways of improving the sound quality of their instruments, e.g. stretching the film tighter, or using a metal rather than plastic bucket. Record and evaluate their findings and use the instruments to compose sound/silence patterns.	• make independent contributions to enquiries and answer simple reasoning questions; recognise similarities and differences in the features of living things and properties of objects consistently. *Example:* working out how to attach the strings to plastic cups when designing a telephone exchange or classifying a selection of stringed instruments. **P8**
	Construct a 'telephone exchange' using plastic cups and string. Investigate different materials, e.g. cotton or plastic threads, or polystyrene or plastic cups, and find out which makes the sound clearer. Find out how many people can be added to the exchange. Play Chinese whispers to check whether every pupil can hear.	Refer to the National Curriculum guidance for science assessment prompts beyond P8.
	Test out walkie-talkies to find out how far away from the classroom they will work. Compare with internal or mobile phones. Which works best?	
Key words Loud Silent Noise Sound Listen Hear Voice See Vibration Move	Use language tapes to listen to and identify different sounds. Make their own tapes of sounds to share with others, e.g. laughing, clapping, singing. Take photographs of the pupils doing the actions and making the sounds to complement the tape. Laminate them to make a game to share.	

Table 9.5 Example of a class teacher's medium-term planning – Key Stage 4

Class Teacher's Medium-term Planning

Subject: Science			PoS: Sc2 Horticulture	
Class: Senior 4		Teacher: Claire	Long-term plan ref.: Year 1, Summer 1	
Lesson	ILO (F)*	Focus skills (A–E)	Activities (Three-part lesson)	
1	All pupils encounter and have access to a broad range of sensory experiences and activities presented in a scientific context through which they may demonstrate awareness; respond and show interest; engage and explore indiscriminately; participate intentionally, and initiate involvement.	Sc1 skill: Planning Key skill: Working with others	Introduction: music cue; key words/symbols. Use gardening books, Internet and other resources to choose suitable plants for a small outdoor garden. Plenary: agree plan and discuss on next steps.	
2		Sc1 skill: Observing Key skill: Improving own learning	Introduction: music cue; key words/symbols. Visit a garden centre to gather ideas. Purchase suitable seeds, plants, compost and propagating kits. Plenary: recap key words; discuss the visit.	
3		Sc1 skill: Planning Key skill: Communication	Introduction: music cue; key words/symbols. Plant and water seeds. Write to parents and local nurseries to request plant donations. Plenary: present their work; discuss next steps.	
4		Sc1 skill: Planning Key skill: Working with others	Introduction: music cue; key words/symbols. Mark and prepare a plot for planting: mix compost, sand, peat; mark out with bark or gravel. Plenary: discuss next steps (e.g. care rota).	
5		Sc1 skill: Recording Key skill: ICT	Introduction: music cue; key words/symbols. Plant out donated plants and pot on seedlings. Produce a care rota and help sheet of the routine. Plenary: reinforce plant care responsibility.	
6		Sc1 skill: Planning Key skill: ICT	Introduction: music cue; key words/symbols. Design and make a set of labels to identify the plants in the garden. Use computer graphics or draw. Plenary: as a group place each label with its plant.	
7		Sc1 skill: Recording Key skill: Improving own learning	Assessment Make pictorial or written lists of the care requirements for their plants. One-to-one support and assessment of pupils' knowledge/skills.	
Science learning outcomes To know the basic requirements to sustain plant life. To use secondary sources to find out about plants.			Cross-curricular links 5B ASDAN bronze	Key words • Seeds • Plant • Garden • Sun • Water • Grow

*ILO(F): Intended learning outcomes (Foundation)

Table 8.8 Example of short-term planning – Key Stage 4

Short-term planning

Subject: Science	PoS: Sc2 Horticulture	Date: 22nd April
Cross-curricular links: ICT, ASDAN		Class: Senior 4

Intended learning outcomes (*Including key skills*)	Key words
Foundation (P1–3) To develop communication and problem-solving skills. To develop cooperative work skills. To be proactive in their exploration of resources. **Access (P4–7)** To contribute to the planning of a miniature garden. To identify parts of a flowering plant. To contribute to group discussions. **Extension (P8–NC1/2)** To use a range of secondary sources to find information for the miniature garden.	• Plant • Grow • Garden • Sun • Water

Activities (*Include differentiation for pupils at Foundation, Access and Extension*)

Introduction: look at basic gardening resources/materials and gardening books.
Split into groups.

Group 1 (Foundation)
Use senses to explore compost (wet/dry), plant pots, seeds etc. Fill and empty containers, spray water.

Group 2 (Access)
Explore a flowering and non-flowering aromatic plant. Find out their names using gardening books or catalogues. Sketch or draw their favourite plants and write or word process a name label for their drawing.

Group 3 (Extension)
Use books or catalogues to select particular plants; use the Internet to find out about them. Print off details

Plenary: regroup; share outcomes, recap the lesson's intention and key words.

Classroom organisation

Group 1	Charlene, Jamie and Usmaa	**Staff**	Hilary and Penny
Group 2	Adam, John and Nathan	**Staff**	Ralph and Mary
Group 3	Ryan, Luke and Rosie	**Staff**	Chris

Resources	IEP targets	
• Potted plants • Gardening books, catalogues and magazines • Compost • Seeds • Water sprays	**Jamie** **Ryan** **Usmaa**	to track objects left to right. to develop mouse skills. to sustain eye contact for 2 seconds.

Resource list for Key Stage 4

Horticulture

Useful website: www.bbc.co.uk/go/learning/int/banner/-/gardening/children/

For natural dye, see: www.nyny.essortment.com/naturaldyeplan_rxll.htm

A simple recording sheet, for example, Figure 9.2.

Figure 9.1 Taking responsibility for plant care during a unit of work on *Horticulture*

Fruit smoothies

Blend soft fruits, e.g. bananas, in an electric blender. Add a little milk to the machine to get it to a pouring consistency or use fresh fruit juice. Try mixing fruits together to make 'smoothie cocktails'.

Sound

Vibraslap – this is a musical percussion instrument available from specialist educational suppliers of musical instruments.

Telephone exchange

Make holes in the bases of two plastic cups. Cut 3 metres of string and thread through each hole. Tie onto paperclips and tape them down. Keep the string taut and the sound will travel. Add other lines by joining 2 metre lengths of strings to the centre. Predict how many 'lines' can be added effectively.

Additional idea

Join plastic cups as above but tie a metal coat hanger in the middle. Put the cups to your ears and ask someone to strike the hanger with a metal spoon. Compare the sound with a plastic coat hanger. Predict which will make the loudest sound.

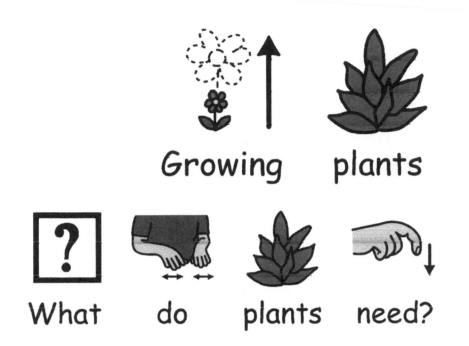

Growing plants

What do plants need?

Name: _____

Figure 9.2 'Growing plants' recording sheet

© Claire Marvin and Chris Stokoe (2003) *Access to Science*, David Fulton Publishers.

CHAPTER TEN

Planning for progression

'Looking through a magic telescope, looking for a creature. Looking for an ant. Ooh! I don't like ants because they come near to me and they tickle me.'

Using a pair of binoculars on a mini-beast hunt. Emma, Year 4

Most teachers, as members of school communities, curriculum planning groups or as individuals, are involved at some stage in the development and evaluation of long- and medium-term curriculum plans. One of the many challenges associated with this task is to produce flexible units of work that provide for and demonstrate appropriate progression from age group to age group and within each of the four key stages. Effective planning, according to the QCA/DfEE (2001b: 14) guidelines, involves 'the careful and deliberate sequencing of curriculum content and experiences which build on previous learning and achievement to promote future learning'.

For pupils with learning difficulties progression is not necessarily only movement up a hierarchical ladder of skills and knowledge. While achievement in a linear dimension should not be overlooked, a lateral understanding of progression should also be adopted. Such a view takes into consideration a wider range of issues and contributes towards preparation for life outside and beyond school. Having a greater understanding of what progress might mean for individual pupils will help teachers to plan for the above. Further support is extended in Table 10.1 where, in order to tease out individual characteristics, the many forms that progression may take are described and exemplified. In practice however they are interrelated and mutually supportive. Teachers should take account of these links in all aspects of planning and seek to combine them in appropriate learning opportunities for their pupils.

For those practitioners who, individually or in collaboration with colleagues, are involved in the development and review of long- and medium-term plans the adoption or adaptation of ready-made materials may help to simplify the complex yet essential task of building in progression of curriculum content and experiences. Depending on individual settings and circumstances there may be much to be gained from examining the increasing amount of material available in hard copy and on the Internet. For example, schemes of work for science are published by the QCA (DfEE/QCA 1998, 2000), EQUALS (EQUALS, in press), the DfES (2002 b, c) and the Cambridgeshire Cluster Group (2001) although this is not a comprehensive list. By using a published scheme as a framework, professional judgement and subject knowledge can then be applied and the content adapted to build on the range of needs, interests and past achievements of pupils in an individual setting.

The recurring unit of work described in Table 10.2 exemplifies the process of planning for effective progression by outlining intended learning outcomes that build on previous achievements of pupils as they progress through the school, while at the same time introducing them to new content and skills. In common with published schemes of work of the same name and, from our experience, those developed in individual or clusters of schools, this unit – *Light and dark* – presents a broad range of learning

Table 10.1 Planning for progression of curriculum content and experiences (adapted from QCA/DfEE 2001b)

Planning for progression of curriculum content and experiences may focus on:	
skill development	for example, from sensory exploration of garden materials and plants, to using available resources to grow plants, to planning and planting a small garden and evaluating the results
breadth of curricular content	including access to new knowledge and understanding, key words and the generalisation of concepts, for example, through a widening focus from learning about light and dark around us, to night and day, to the Earth beyond
a range of contexts for learning	so that activities, resources and environments are appropriate to pupils' ages, interests, achievements and previous experiences. For example, from active exploration of materials using all available senses, to carrying out investigations, such as finding out the best materials for walking safely on a slippery surface
a range of teaching approaches	including playful activities for all age groups
strategies for independence	so that learners are enabled to move away from dependence to independence, for example, utilising their knowledge about living things to care for pets
negotiated learning	where pupils are encouraged to take a greater part in the learning process. The skills associated with scientific enquiry support this aspect of progress
application of skills, knowledge and understanding in a widening environment	for example, following safety rules applied to the use of tools at school – at home, at college and at work

outcomes. It also demonstrates the tracking back of scientific ideas described as an effective method of ensuring appropriate learning for pupils with special educational needs in the *Key Stage 3 National Strategy* framework for science (DfES 2002a).

Developed for its flexibility of content, for example, the opportunity but not the necessity, to include knowledge and understanding from several strands of *Physical processes* (Sc4) across several key stages, the unit also provides meaningful reasons to practise skills and apply knowledge with increasing independence in practical situations in preparation for adult life. This is demonstrated by a change in focus from key stage to key stage, for example, at Key Stage 1 an emphasis on experiencing and exploring light and dark and its association with night and day; at Key Stage 4 on life skills, for example, being safe in the sun, recognising the suitability of light sources for different activities and links to everyday life.

In Key Stages 3 and 4 in particular some parts of the programmes of study for science will prove too demanding for pupils with learning difficulties, for example, aspects of *Patterns of behaviour* (Sc3) and *The Earth and beyond* (Sc4). However, we believe that all pupils should access the rich and varied content included in later key stages. Such opportunities create breadth and depth of experience and help to maintain pupils' curiosity and enthusiasm for science. While the content dimension of some units may be purely experiential, challenging scientific activities can provide a context for meaningful learning that contributes towards preparation for life outside and beyond school, for example in the areas of key skills and daily living skills. For this reason finding out about aspects of *The Earth and beyond* (Sc4), that involves the development and application of skills associated with accessing and using secondary sources, is included in Table 10.2.

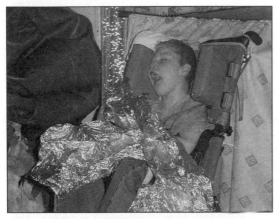

10.1a Responding to shiny materials and lighting effects

10.1b Focusing on light

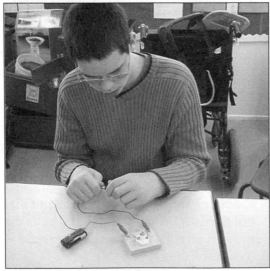

10.1c Consolidating knowledge, skills and understanding from a previous unit of work on *Electricity*

10.1d Come and join me in the dark!

Figure 10.1 *Light and dark* – the unit of work in action

Table 10.2 Light and dark: progression in curriculum content and experiences

Key Stage 1	Key Stage 2
Pupils may:	Pupils may:
• Experience and respond to a broad range of sensory and play-focused activities related to light and dark.	• Explore and investigate within a broad range of sensory and play-focused activities relating to light and dark and day and night.
• Anticipate and respond to obvious contrasts of light and dark.	• Communicate what will happen when a light source is activated.
• Locate the source of a light and track movement.	• Recognise and identify the source of a light and find out how it is powered.
• Explore and use simple switches to operate lighting effects.	• Recognise similarities and differences in artificial light sources and group them to given criteria, for example, torches, lamps, candles, overhead projector.
• Begin to recognise light and dark across a range of familiar contexts.	• Know that light is needed for seeing things. Identify light and dark places and make the connection to day and night.
• Observe shadows and explore the effects of light with other materials, for example, shiny, transparent, opaque, translucent.	• Observe, recognise and comment on the movement of shadows created by natural and artificial light.
• Know when the Sun is out and when it goes behind a cloud.	• Observe that light shines through some materials and not others.
	• Know that the Sun is a source of light and use a familiar range of simple secondary sources to find out about it.

Table 10.2 continued

Key Stage 3	Key Stage 4
Pupils may:	Pupils may:
• Explore and investigate a broad range of sensory and playful materials and phenomena related to light and dark and the Earth and beyond.	• Explore and investigate a broad range of sensory and playful materials and phenomena related to light and dark and the Earth and beyond. Link existing knowledge, skills and understanding to everyday events.
• Identify and name sources of light, including the Sun, and group them to given criteria, for example, battery-operated/mains-operated devices; natural/artificial light sources.	• Identify activities that generally happen in the day and at night and explain why.
• Know that some light sources are more effective than others and that they show up best at night.	• Refer to and use evidence to select appropriate light sources for different activities. Operate them independently and begin to give reasons for selection.
• Follow basic health and safety rules related to natural and artificial light sources, for example, not to look directly at the Sun, to switch off both the electrical appliance and the socket before plugging in or unplugging.	• Know that darkness is the absence of light.
• Participate in the construction and use of a simple electrical circuit to power a light source.	• Understand that light sources can be powered in different ways, recall health and safety rules that apply to their use and take action to control risks to themselves and others.
• Begin to recognise the importance of the Sun and how it sustains life.	• From given components know how to construct a simple electrical circuit to power a light source and observe what happens when the circuit is broken.
• Observe the apparent movement of the Sun and measure the effect on shadows.	• Know why the Sun is an essential factor in sustaining life on Earth and predict outcomes should the Sun cease to exist.
• Use a range of secondary sources to observe: the spherical nature of the Earth, Sun and Moon; the movement of the Earth on its own axis and its connection to day and night; our planet Earth in relation to other planets.	• Predict from previous experience a few materials that will form a shadow and some through which light will pass.
	• Know that shadows are formed when light is blocked.
	• Use an increasing range of secondary sources in a variety of settings to research topics linked to the unit of work, for example, the solar system; how light travels; day and night.

Conclusion – meeting the challenge

For pupils with learning difficulties, as for all pupils, it is our belief that with skilful organisation, creative yet conscientious planning and a knowledge of the individual learner, the routes to accessing the science curriculum are very clearly open. Learning science, according to the QCA/DfEE (2001a: 4) guidelines, gives all pupils the opportunity to think and learn, and develop an interest in, and curiosity about, the world around them through exploratory and investigative experiences and activities. A curriculum that is accessible and that provides all pupils, without exception, with the opportunity to participate in learning at an appropriate level and to experience success, is an essential foundation for inclusion.

Throughout this book it is argued that the processes, concepts, understandings and skills of the science programmes of study offer a genuine and exciting path to learning. In addition, the scientific method can be seen as a basis for all kinds of learning about the world, and includes essential skills which run through most educational experiences for all learners. Essentially science is a versatile subject through which practitioners may focus on areas of learning that are priorities for individual and groups of pupils. Learners will be working simultaneously towards a range of goals, both cross-curricular and subject-focused.

The primary task of making access to science a practical reality and its content exciting, meaningful and relevant, lies with every practitioner in every school setting. It is our intention in this book to demonstrate those possibilities through the exemplification of effective planning and the promotion of enthusiastic teaching. We, as teachers, need to support and encourage our pupils to explore and to investigate, to use all their available senses, to problem solve and to affect and observe what happens. This involves not so much the process of leading them to discover what is out there but rather, as Bruner (1971) suggests, their discovering what is in their own heads. Furthermore we need to be learners alongside our pupils, infecting them with our interest and our curiosity. To this end we should look afresh at the opportunities we provide for active styles of learning which, we believe, are best delivered within a playful, motivating and exciting environment. Such an environment will provide new experiences and, perhaps most crucially, opportunities for learning about science through play.

Play is a person's way of understanding the world, and its contents and contexts, in order to gain an awareness of both one's place in that world and one's control over it. It is a powerful tool for learning. Everyone must play in order to build concepts and understandings in every area of their world and, therefore, in every curriculum subject. Moyles (1989: 86) takes a pragmatic stance on this issue:

> because play is an approach it is within subjects that one should look to play as a means of teaching and learning rather than as a separate entity. Because of the relevance and motivation of play to children play must pervade how teachers present learning activities, not sit as an uncomfortable and somewhat suspect activity in itself.

Science is a subject that is both accessible and relevant to all pupils. It has potential to enrich the curriculum and provide interesting contexts for learning. Yet the challenge remains of maintaining a well-rounded and inclusive curriculum that provides access to all subjects, including science, while at the same time addressing the needs of individual pupils. Despite this difficult task teachers should not lose sight of the opportunity, through imaginative and creative teaching, to share enthusiasm for science with their pupils. In this way they will all enjoy access to the subject in ways which stimulate curiosity and excite them to learn. It is our intention that this book provides practical support and inspiration to all who are working towards a genuinely inclusive curriculum.

Resources

Internet sites

www.issen.org.uk

This site was established as part of the Inclusive Science and Special Educational Needs Project. Funded by the Department for Education and Skills (DfES) through the SEN Small Programmes Fund the project represents a collaboration between the Association for Science Education (ASE) and the National Association for Special Educational Needs (NASEN). It aims to strengthen the links between ASE and NASEN in their support for teachers and other professionals working with pupils with special educational needs in mainstream and specialist settings. To this end the web pages facilitate networking and the sharing of good practice, ideas and resources between teachers, organisations and other interested individuals. The site is continually updated and includes numerous links to other relevant sites.

Users can subscribe to the ISSEN email discussion group by sending an email to: <issen-request@freelists.org> with 'subscribe' in the subject field.

www.azteachscience.co.uk/trust/cambridge.htm

Sponsored by the AstraZeneca Teaching Trust this very useful site features materials developed by members of the Cambridgeshire SEN Science Project. Led by a group of special school practitioners and known as STRATA (Science To Raise And Track Achievement) the outcome is a comprehensive scheme of work and an assessment and recording framework for science that is 'both age-appropriate and sufficient to meet the needs of the whole ability range' (Cambridgeshire Cluster Group Project 2001).

www.planet-science.com

Planet Science is a campaign focused particularly on young people that aims to stimulate the imagination about science and technology. With extensive links to other sites the website features information on events, projects and resource giveaways that include *The Little Book of Experiments* – free to all primary schools.

www.priorywoods.middlesborough.sch.uk/resources

One of several special school sites with curriculum policies and schemes of work available to download.

www.standards.dfes.gov.uk

The Department for Education and Skills (DfES) site includes an exemplar scheme of work for science at Key Stage 1 and 2 in addition to information and practical materials for the Key Stage 3 National Strategy Framework for teaching science. There are sample science units available to download – *Heating and cooling* and *Resistance to movement* – to support the work of teachers who are concerned with planning science-focused experiences and activities for pupils with learning difficulties.

www.becta.org.uk/inclusion/discussion/index.html

The British Educational Communications and Technology agency (BECTa) has worked closely with groups of teachers, advisory staff, teacher trainers and researchers to set up a range of focused discussion areas. The majority of these use email and are known as mailing lists that are free to join. They intend to provide a forum for the sharing of ideas, views and information in addition to encouraging ongoing professional development with colleagues.

Participants send a message to a central email address and that message is then sent to everyone who has 'signed up' to be a member of the list.

(i) SLD-forum

A mailing list for professionals involved in the education of learners with severe and profound and multiple learning difficulties.

To join the list send the following message to: <majordomo@ngfl.gov.uk>
Subject: (leave blank)
Body of message: subscribe sld-forum

(ii) senco-forum

A mailing list for special educational needs coordinators (SENCOs), those in local authority services and other interested parties.

To join the list send the following message to: <majordomo@ngfl.gov.uk>
Subject: (leave blank)
Body of message: subscribe senco-forum

www.hawkin.com

The website of Hawkin & Co., St Margaret, Harleston, Norfolk IP20 0HN
Tel: 01986 782536 Fax: 01986 782468
email: sales@hawkin.com

Hawkin & Co. supply reasonably priced gadgets, gizmos and toys that are described in the recent catalogue *Hawkin's Bazaar 2003* as, 'Things you thought had gone for ever. Things you never knew existed.' Useful resources that we thought had gone for ever include: baking-powder powered diving submarines @ £2.99 and traditional metal humming tops @ £7.99.

Books and periodicals

Any particular list of science books and periodicals is unlikely to meet the individual needs of the range of professionals working with pupils with learning difficulties. Science subject leaders and LEA advisers are best placed to recommend publications relevant to particular circumstances and settings. Nevertheless, we are suggesting one book that, in our opinion, is particularly useful:

> Hollins, M. and Whitby, V. with Lander, L., Parson, B. and Williams, M. (2001) *Progression in Primary Science. A guide to the nature and practice of science in Key Stage 1 and 2*, 2nd edn. London: David Fulton Publishers.

This book is designed to enable students in initial teacher education and newly qualified teachers to make effective and informed links between scientific knowledge and its application for pupils in primary classrooms. Also it may be useful as a reference book for science leaders and teachers who regard themselves as non-specialists in the subject. Using straightforward language and many examples from mainstream classroom practice the authors offer a clear and accessible guide to the main concepts set out in the science programme of study for Key Stages 1 and 2 (DfEE/QCA 1999a).

Photographs and images

Free photographs and images are available on the Internet but access to many sites is restricted to subscribers. A useful place to start is http://images.google.com/ or, for further inspiration, try an email group (see 'Internet sites' and 'Useful addresses and telephone numbers').

Copyright laws should be observed when consulting large format picture books. Images available on CD-ROMS are usually copyright-free.

Signs and symbols

Makaton Vocabulary Development Project

For information on the Makaton Vocabulary Development Project (materials and training in the use of signs and symbols) contact:

The Makaton Vocabulary Development Project, 31 Firwood Drive, Camberley, Surrey GU15 3QD
Tel: 01276 61390 Fax: 01276 681368
email: mvdp@makaton.org   website: www.makaton.org

In addition to the *Makaton Core Vocabulary* which is widely used in schools and centres for adults with learning difficulties the *National Curriculum Series Part 1* provides an additional vocabulary that covers aspects of the National Curriculum subject areas including science. To this can be added further booklets relevant to science, for example, *Animals, Transport and Vehicles*.

Electrical Safety in Symbols for Special Needs

To obtain a copy of *Electrical Safety in Symbols for Special Needs* order direct from:
Understanding Energy, 30 Millbank, London SW1P 4RD

Tel: 020 7963 5839

Safety issues both inside and outside the home are highlighted in this pack using words, Makaton symbols and signs to help pupils and adults understand essential safety messages. Order code: EC237/MAK

Widgit Software Ltd

Resource Development and Training, Widgit Software Ltd, 124 Cambridge Science Park, Milton Rd, Cambridge CB4 0ZS
Tel: 01223 425558 Fax: 01223 425349
email: imogen@widgit.com   website: www.widgit.com

Widgit Software Ltd provides symbol software for people who require support in communication and literacy. The recently completed Rebus Symbol Development Project was established to review the whole symbol set with a view to developing consistency. The resulting software package is now available. In addition a new website – www.symbolworld.org – aimed at symbol users in schools, gives appropriate content to symbol and includes scientific content.

Useful addresses and telephone numbers

DfES publications

Tel: 0845 60 222 60   Fax: 0845 60 333 60   Textphone: 0845 60 555 60
email: dfes@prolog.uk.com   website: www.dfes.gov.uk

The Association for Science Education (ASE)

ASE, College Lane, Hatfield, Herts AL10 9AA
Tel: 01707 283000   Fax: 01707 266532
email: membership@ase.org.uk/booksales@ase.org.uk   website: www.ase.org.uk

EQUALS

EQUALS, PO Box 107, North Shields, Tyne and Wear NE30 2YG
Tel/Fax: 0191 272 8600
email: admin@equals.co.uk   website: www.equals.co.uk

A national organisation that seeks to support and encourage ongoing critical debate about the needs of pupils with severe and profound and multiple learning difficulties. Extensive planning and assessment materials are available for purchase and national conferences are arranged in support of teachers and other professionals who work in a range of settings.

Qualifications and Curriculum Authority (QCA)

QCA, 83 Piccadilly, London W1J 8QA
Tel: customer services team 020 7509 5556
Tel: QCA publication 01787 884444   Fax: 01787 312950
email: info@qca.org.uk   website: www.qca.org.uk

Accreditation schemes

Accreditation of Life and Living (ALL)

ALL, OCR (Oxford, Cambridge and RSA Examinations), Westwood Way, Coventry CV4 8JQ
Tel: 02476 470033   Fax: 02476 421944

email: cib@ocr.org.uk   website: www.ocr.org.uk

Accreditation of Life and Living is an assessed award for Key Stage 4+ pupils with severe and profound and multiple learning difficulties. It offers a flexible qualification structure tailored to the needs of those taking part. The Key Skill modules are designed to be delivered in the context of the Life and Living Skills modules. There is minimal scientific content.

Award Scheme Development and Accreditation Network (ASDAN)

ASDAN, Wainbrook House, Hudds Vale Rd, St George, Bristol BS5 7HY
Tel: 0117 941 1126   Fax: 0117 935 1112
email: info@asdan.co.uk   website: www.asdan.co.uk

Linked with the University of the West of England in Bristol this award scheme for secondary phase pupils offers learner-centred opportunities to negotiate a curriculum that is modular and activity based. Achievement is recorded in the context of programmes of study for Key Stage 4 National Curriculum subjects, complemented by activities linked to the skills associated with independent living.

Overview

A brief overview of the confusing array of accrediting and validating organisations that approve courses, programmes of study and learning packages can be found in: Parkyn, L. (2002) 'Accreditation – jumping through hoops or recognising and rewarding achievement?' *Special Children* **150**, 38–40.

Health and safety

Consortium of Local Education Authorities for the Provision of Science Services (CLEAPSS)

The CLEAPSS School Science Service, Brunel University, Uxbridge UP8 3PH
Tel: (helpline) 01895 251496   Fax: 01895 814372
email: science@cleapss.org.uk   website: www.cleapss.org.uk

The CLEAPSS School Science Service is a nation-wide advisory body to which all eligible LEAs throughout the British Isles – excluding Scotland – belong. One of its roles is to advise on health and safety for practical science and technology in schools and to provide associated publications and training. The helpline is free to teachers and others where the education authority is a member, or to those working in schools that are associate members.

Scottish Schools Equipment Research Centre (SSERC)

SSERC, St Mary's Building, 23 Holyrood Rd, Edinburgh EH8 8AE
Tel: 0131 558 8180   Fax: 0131 558 8191
email: sts@sserc.org.uk   website: www.sserc.org.uk

An organisation for LEAs, their schools and other subscribing organisations in Scotland. It offers similar support to that of CLEAPSS.

Association of Science (ASE) publications

see address under 'Useful addresses and telephone numbers'

In addition to other services the association publishes extensively on health and safety issues. A useful publication is:

ASE (2001) *Be Safe! Health and safety in primary school science and technology*, 3rd edn. Hatfield, Herts: ASE.

Recipes

There are many methods for making dough but they are mostly variations on three basic recipes described below (adapted from Whitebread, D. (ed.) (1996) *Teaching and Learning in the Early Years*. London: Routledge). Pupils can make their own discoveries about this undervalued 'scientific' resource through sensory exploration.

Cooked dough

2 cups plain four
1 cup salt
2 cups water
2 tbsp cooking oil
2 tsp cream of tartar
colouring (optional)

Cook all ingredients in a saucepan over low heat, stirring continuously. For solid colour, mix the food colouring with the water before adding, or for a marbled effect, add separately. Remove from heat when the mixture leaves sides of the pan. Knead, adding any products designed to add texture and store in an airtight container.

Stretchy dough

1.5 kg self-raising flour
500 ml water

Mix the ingredients together. The mixture will require a lot of kneading. The longer it is kneaded the stretchier it becomes!

Pastry/salt dough

2 cups plain flour
1 cup salt
$\frac{1}{4}$ cup of tepid water
1 tbsp cooking oil

Mix the flour and salt before adding the water. Oil can be added to give a smoother texture and a glossy appearance. Knead thoroughly. After modelling, dry in a very low oven for at least 12 hours.

Planning sheets

Blank planning sheet formats for medium-term planning for subject leaders and class teachers and for short-term planning are available for photocopying (Tables R1–R3).

Table R.1 Subject leader's medium-term planning sheet

Subject Leader's Medium-term Planning

Key Stage:	Subject:	PoS:	Curriculum links:	L-TP reference:
Intended learning outcomes	Activities		Assessment prompts	

Table R.2 Class teacher's medium-term planning sheet

Class Teacher's Medium-term Planning

Subject:			PoS:
Class:		Teacher:	Long-term plan ref.:
Lesson	**ILO (F)***	**Focus skills (A–E)**	**Activities** *(Three-part lesson)*
1	All pupils encounter and have access to a broad range of sensory experiences and activities presented in a subject-specific context through which they may demonstrate awareness; respond and show interest; engage and explore indiscriminately; participate intentionally, and initiate involvement.	Sc1 skill: Key skill:	
2		Sc1 skill: Key skill:	
3		Sc1 skill: Key skill:	
4		Sc1 skill: Key skill:	
5		Sc1 skill: Key skill:	
6		Sc1 skill: Key skill:	
7		Sc1 skill: Key skill:	**Assessment**

Learning outcomes	**Cross-curricular links**	**Key words**

*ILO(F): Intended learning outcomes (Foundation)

Table R.3 Short-term planning sheet

Short-term planning

Subject:	PoS:	Date:
Cross-curricular links:		Class:

Intended learning outcomes (*Including key skills*) **Foundation (P1–3)** **Access (P4–7)** **Extension (P8–NC1/2)**	**Key words** • • • • •

Activities (*Include differentiation for pupils at Foundation, Access and Extension*)

Introduction:

Group 1 (Foundation)

Group 2 (Access)

Group 3 (Extension)

Plenary:

Classroom organisation

Group 1	Staff
Group 2	Staff
Group 3	Staff

Resources • • • • •	**IEP targets**

References

Alexander, R., Rose, J. and Woodhead, C. (1992) *Curriculum Organisation and Classroom Practice in Primary Schools. A discussion paper.* London: DES.

Ashman, A. F. and Conway, R. N. F. (1989) *Cognitive Strategies for Special Education.* London: Routledge.

Bell, D. (1998) 'Accessing science: challenges faced by teachers of children with learning difficulties in primary schools', *Support for Learning* **13**(1), 26–31.

Bell, D. (2002) 'Making science inclusive: providing effective learning opportunities for children with learning difficulties', *Support for Learning* **17**(4), 156–61.

Bennett, S. N. and Carré, C. G. (1993) *Learning to Teach.* London: Routledge.

Both, K. (1997) 'Exploring sensibility and wonder', in Härnqvist, K. and Burgen, A. (eds) *Growing Up with Science*, 144–63. London: Jessica Kingsley.

Bruner, J. S. (1971) *The Relevance of Education.* Cambridge, MA: Harvard University Press.

Bruner, J. S. (1972) 'The nature and uses of immaturity', *American Psychologist* **27**, 1–28.

Burrows, N. (2000) 'Play, leisure and age-appropriateness', *PMLD Link* **12**(3), 27–8.

Byers, R. (1999) 'Experience and achievement: initiatives in curriculum development for pupils with severe and profound and multiple learning difficulties', *British Journal of Special Education* **26**(4), 184–8.

Byers, R. and Rose, R. (1996) *Planning the Curriculum for Pupils with Special Educational Needs.* London: David Fulton Publishers.

Cambridgeshire Cluster Group Project (2001) *Scheme of Work* [WWW] 2001. Http://www.azteachscience.co.uk/trust/cambridge/schemeofwork.htm

Carpenter, B. and Ashdown, R. (2001) 'Enabling access', in Carpenter, B., Ashdown, R. and Bovair, K. (eds) *Enabling Access. Effective teaching and learning for pupils with learning difficulties*, 2nd edn, 1–14. London: David Fulton Publishers.

Collis, M. and Lacey, P. (1996) *Interactive Approaches to Teaching.* London: David Fulton Publishers.

Coltman, P. (1996) 'In search of the Elephant's Child', in Whitebread, D. (ed.) *Teaching and Learning in the Early Years*, 243–54. London: Routledge.

Coupe O'Kane, J. and Goldbart, J. (eds) (1996) *Whose Choice? Contentious issues for those working with people with learning difficulties.* London: David Fulton Publishers.

Coupe O'Kane, J. and Smith, B. (eds) (1994) *Taking Control. Enabling people with learning difficulties.* London: David Fulton Publishers.

(DES) Department of Education and Science (1985) *Science 5–16. A Statement of Policy.* London: HMSO.

(DES) Department of Education and Science (1988) The Education Reform Act. London: HMSO.

DfE (1995) *The National Curriculum.* London: HMSO.

DfEE/QCA (1998) *A Scheme of Work for Key Stages 1 and 2. Science.* London: QCA.

DfEE/QCA (1999a) *Science. The National Curriculum for England.* London: DfEE/QCA.

DfEE/QCA (1999b) *The National Curriculum. Handbook for primary teachers in England.* London: DfEE/QCA.

DfEE/QCA (2000) *A Scheme of Work for Key Stages 1 and 2. Science. Teacher's guide. Update.* London: QCA.

DfES (2002a) *Key Stage 3 National Strategy. Launch of the science strand in special schools and units.* London: DfES.

DfES (2002b) *Key Stage 3 National Strategy. Sample science units to support pupils with special educational needs. Heating and cooling.* London: DfES.

DfES (2002c) *Key Stage 3 National Strategy. Sample science units to support pupils with special educational needs. Resistance to movement.* London: DfES.

Donaldson, M. (1978) *Children's Minds.* London: Fontana Press.

Dorchester Curriculum Group (2002) *Towards a Curriculum for All. A practical guide for developing an inclusive curriculum for pupils attaining significantly below age-related expectations.* London: David Fulton Publishers.

EQUALS (in press) *Science for Pupils with Learning Difficulties.* North Shields, Tyne and Wear: EQUALS.

Farrell, P. (1997) *Teaching Pupils with Learning Difficulties. Strategies and solutions.* London: Cassell.

Fisher, R. (1990) *Teaching Children to Think.* Hemel Hempstead: Blackwell/Simon and Schuster Publishers.

Fisher, R. (1995) *Teaching Children to Learn.* Cheltenham: Stanley Thornes.

Fontana, D. (1995) *Psychology for Teachers,* 3rd edn. Basingstoke, Hampshire: Macmillan Press.

Hollins, M. and Whitby, V. (2001) *Progression in Primary Science. A guide to the nature and practice of science in Key Stages 1 and 2,* 2nd edn. London: David Fulton Publishers.

Howe, L. (1992) 'Science' in Bovair, K., Carpenter, B. and Upton, G. (eds) *Special Curricula Needs,* 11–28. London: David Fulton Publishers.

HMI (1986) *A Survey of Science in Special Education.* London: HMSO.

HMI (1990) *Education Observed. Special needs issues.* London: HMSO.

Jones, L. and Skelton, S. (1993) *Science for All,* 2nd edn. London: David Fulton Publishers.

Jordan, R. and Libby, S. (1997) 'Developing and using play in the curriculum', in Powell, S. and Jordan, R. (eds) *Autism and Learning. A guide to good practice,* 22–45. London: David Fulton Publishers.

Kelly, P. (1997) 'Consolidating science in primary education', in Härnqvist, K. and Burgen, A. (eds) *Growing Up with Science*, 250–65. London: Jessica Kingsley Publishers.

Lacey, P. (2001) 'Music', in Carpenter, B., Ashdown, R. and Bovair, K. (eds) *Enabling Access. Effective teaching and learning for pupils with learning difficulties*, 2nd edn, 120–32. London: David Fulton Publishers.

Lawson, H., Marvin, C. and Pratt, A. (2001) 'Planning, teaching and assessing the curriculum for pupils with learning difficulties: an introduction and overview', *Support for Learning* **16**(4), 162–7.

Magorian, M. (1983) *Goodnight Mr Tom*. London: Penguin Books.

Marshall, C. and Palacio, D. (1997) 'Science', in Ashcroft, K. and Palacio, D. (eds) *Implementing the Primary Curriculum. A teacher's guide*, 66–84. London: Falmer.

Marvin, C. (1998) 'Teaching and learning for children with PMLD', in Lacey, P. and Ouvry, C. (eds) *People with PMLD. A collaborative approach to meeting complex needs*, 117–29. London: David Fulton Publishers.

Mittler, P. (2001) 'Preparing for self-advocacy', in Carpenter, B., Ashdown, R. and Bovair, K. (eds) *Enabling Access. Effective teaching and learning for pupils with learning difficulties*, 2nd edn, 328–45. London: David Fulton Publishers.

Moyles, J. (1989) *Just Playing? The role and status of play in early childhood education*. Buckingham: Open University Press.

NCC (National Curriculum Council) (1992a) *Curriculum Guidance 9. The National Curriculum and pupils with severe learning difficulties*. York: National Curriculum Council.

NCC (National Curriculum Council) (1992b) *Curriculum Guidance 10. Teaching science to pupils with special educational needs*. York: National Curriculum Council.

Nind, M. and Hewett, D. (1994) *Access to Communication. Developing the basics of communication with people with severe learning difficulties through Intensive Interaction*. London: David Fulton Publishers.

Ofsted (1998) *Standards in the Primary Curriculum 1996–97*. London: Ofsted.

Ofsted (2001) *Annual Report of HM Chief Inspector of Schools 1998/99*. London: The Stationery Office.

Ofsted (2002) *The Curriculum in Successful Primary Schools*. London: Ofsted.

QCA/DfEE (1999) *Early Learning Goals*. London: QCA.

QCA/DfEE (2000) *Curriculum Guidance for the Foundation Stage*. London: QCA.

QCA/DfEE (2001a) *Planning, Teaching and Assessing the Curriculum for Pupils with Learning Difficulties. Science*. London: QCA.

QCA/DfEE (2001b) *Planning, Teaching and Assessing the Curriculum for Pupils with Learning Difficulties. General guidelines*. London: QCA.

QCA/DfEE (2001c) *Planning, Teaching and Assessing the Curriculum for Pupils with Learning Difficulties. Developing skills*. London: QCA.

QCA/DfEE (2001d) *Supporting the Target Setting Process* (revised March 2001). London: DfEE.

Ritchie, R. (2001) 'Science', in Carpenter, B., Ashdown, R. and Bovair, K. (eds) *Enabling Access. Effective teaching and learning for pupils with learning difficulties*, 2nd edn, 52–65. London: David Fulton Publishers.

Russell, T., Qualter, A., Mcguigan, L. and Hughes, A. (1994) *Evaluation and Implementation of Science in the National Curriculum at Key Stages 1, 2 and 3.* London: SCAA.

SCAA (School Curriculum and Assessment Authority) (1996) *Planning the Curriculum for Pupils with Profound and Multiple Learning Difficulties.* London: SCAA.

Sherratt, D. and Peter, M. (2002) *Developing Play and Drama in Children with Autistic Spectrum Disorders.* London: David Fulton Publishers.

Sylva, K., Bruner, J. S. and Genova, P. (1974) 'The role of play in the problem-solving of children 3–5 years old', in Bruner, J. S., Jolly, A. and Sylva, K. (eds) (1976) *Play*, 244–57. Harmondsworth, Middlesex: Penguin.

Teacher Training Agency (TTA) (1998) *National Standards for Subject Leaders.* London: Teacher Training Agency.

Tilstone, C., Lacey, P., Porter, J. and Robertson, C. (2000) *Pupils with Learning Difficulties in Mainstream Schools.* London: David Fulton Publishers.

Turner, A. (2002) *Access to History.* London: David Fulton Publishers.

Vygotsky, L. S. (1978) *Mind in Society. The development of higher psychological processes.* Cambridge, MA: Harvard University Press.

Wood, D. (1998) *How Children Think and Learn*, 2nd edn. Oxford: Blackwell Publishers.

Wood, E. and Attfield, J. (1996) *Play, Learning and the Early Childhood Curriculum.* London: Paul Chapman Publishing.

Wood, E. and Bennett, N. (1997) 'The rhetoric and reality of play: teachers' thinking and classroom practice', *Early Years* **17**(2), 22–7.

Index

access
  equality of 33
access stage, 31, 32, 33,
  48–50
accreditation 3
ASDAN 29, 36
assessment 34
  prompts 32
  summative 34

cross-curricular links 9, 33
  and skills 7
curriculum *see also* science
  curriculum
  balance 2, 3
  components 2
  inclusive vii
  links 16, 30
  model 8
  planning 138
  requirements 3

differentiation 31, 33, 34, 44

early learning goals 3, 29
experiences and opportunities
  at Key Stage 1 55
  at Key Stage 2 77
  at Key Stage 3 105
  at Key Stage 4 125
extension stage 31, 32, 33,
  51–3

flexibility of thought
  Bruner's theory of 24, 25–6
foundation stage 31, 32, 33,
  45–7

health and safety ix, 149

inclusion 1
individual education plans
  (IEPs) 32, 34
interactive display 27

key skills 7, 12
  additional skills 12
Key Stage 3 *National Strategy*
  framework for teaching
  science 29, 139
key words 32
knowledge and understanding
  5, 7, 29

learning
  active 17
  intended learning outcomes
    31, 32
  opportunities 138
  science-focused 39
learning to learn 7
life processes and living things
  5

materials and their properties 5
modelling 18, 23, 26, 27, 42

National Curriculum viii, 1, 2,
  7, 9, 31, 39

Ofsted 1, 7

performance descriptions (P
  levels) viii
physical processes 5
planning *see also* curriculum
  effective 29
  long-term 3, 29, 30
  medium-term viii, 29, 30,
    32, 33, 34
  for progression viii, 138
  for scientific enquiry 44
  short-term 29, 34
  units of work viii
play, 17, 22
  age-appropriate 19
  contexts of 23
  exploratory 26
  importance of 19
  parallel 23
  playful experiences 24
  playful nature of science 12
practical activities 40
problem solving 3, 5, 24
programmes of study 3, 5, 7,
  30, 39
  content 3
  process 3
progression 29, 30, 34, 138
  planning for *see* planning
prompt sheet 18, 19, 20, 21
pupils
  with autistic spectrum
    disorder 33, 43
  interests of 7
  mainstream 7
  past experiences of 7

primary 7
  with profound and multiple
    learning difficulties 29,
    31, 36
  secondary 7
  with severe learning
    difficulties 29, 36

questioning 5, 17, 18
  higher order 18

sabotage 28
scheme of work 8
science curriculum *see also*
  curriculum
  content dimension of 3, 7
  process dimension of 3
science leader 7, 8, 9, 16
science skills 39, 40, 45–53
  development of 41
  evaluation 39, 44
  investigation 17, 39, 42, 44
  observation 5, 17
  planning 39
  recording 27, 39
science weeks 30, 31
scientific enquiry 3, 4, 5, 6,
  17, 28, 33, 40, 44
senses 15, 17
  sensory circus 15
  sensory dimension 17
  sensory process 2
subject
  balance 2
  host 12
  knowledge 1, 7
  leader 8, 30

target setting 5
teaching
  activities and experiences
    31, 32, 34
  approaches 17, 23, 27
  methods of 34
terminology viii–ix
thinking and learning 2, 18
tracking back 29, 139

unit of work, 32, 37, 138 *see
  also* programme of study

zone of proximal development
  23, 24